The Working Woman's Guide to Breastfeeding

by Anne Price
and Nancy Dana

Meadowbrook
Distributed by Simon and Schuster
New York

Published by Meadowbrook, Inc., 18318 Minnetonka Boulevard, Deephaven, MN 55391

Editor: Susan Freese
Production: Nanci Stoddard
Art Direction: Mary Foster
Keylining: Bob Flaten, Scott Stoddard, Jerome Beckley
Text Design: Nanci Stoddard
Cover Design: Mary Foster
Illustrations: Patricia Carey
Photography: Glen Silker Studios

Library of Congress Cataloging-in-Publication Data

Price, Anne.
  The working woman's guide to breastfeeding.

  Includes index.
  1. Breast feeding. 2. Women—Employment.
I. Dana, Nancy.   II. Title. RJ216.P6976 1987   649.33   87-5548
ISBN 0-671-63624-3

87 88 89 90 10 9 8 7 6 5 4 3 2 1
Printed in the United States of America

The Foreword, pp. vii-viii, is reprinted with permission of Lynn Redgrave. The information on positioning the baby for nursing, pp. 18-21, is used with permission of Kittie Frantz. Technique 1 of hand expression, pp. 80-81, is used with permission of Jo Ann Touchton. Technique 2 of hand expression, pp. 82-87, is used with permission of Chele Marmet.

We gratefully acknowledge:

Dr. Usha Varma, for her initial suggestion that a book like this needed to be written and that we were the people to do it.

Chele Marmet, Kittie Frantz, and Jo Ann Touchton, for all the work they have done to help women breastfeeding and for lending their knowledge and support to us.

Our children—Lev, Mikki, and Gabriel Price and Tad and Tucker Bamford—for their belief in us and their love, support, and encouragement from the moment of conception through the labor and birth of this project.

The many other people who have offered help, information, advice, and support, such as all the women who related their personal experiences and answered our questionnaire. We can't possibly thank them all individually here, but we do hope that they will accept our thanks for their important collective contribution to this effort to help other women.

Contents

Foreword

When my third baby, Annabel, was about six months old, my husband and I took her, as we often did, to a party. When she woke during the evening, I sat in our host's bedroom nursing her. Soon one of the guests came in. "Do you mind if I watch?" she asked. "I've never seen a woman breastfeed a baby before." This woman had two children, but she said it had never occurred to her to breastfeed them, and no one had suggested it, either.

Living as we do, in a time when the extended family is often scattered, when most of this generation's mothers were bottlefed, the new mother looks around in vain for help and guidance and examples of breastfeeding as a simple, natural part of bringing up her baby.

Breastfeeding provides more than the best food. It is more than the most convenient method. It is the beginning of the language of love. Through this special bond with the mother, the baby first learns to receive love and in doing so grows to be a person who can love in return.

When my first child was born [nearly twenty] years ago, I breastfed him not without some problems. How I wish I'd had this book then. I knew nothing of the growth spurts that made him need to nurse more frequently. When these would happen, I'd assume I didn't have enough milk, and instead of nursing him more often to build up the supply, I gave him a bottle. The vicious circle began. No one that I knew was breastfeeding, my doctor recommended supplementing with a bottle, and my mother had raised me at a time when you nursed at four-hour intervals and that was that. More might spoil the baby!

When he was five months old I had to do a movie in Singapore. He was too young to have the required immunization shots and, fool that I was, I stopped nursing and left him behind. Little did I know that had I kept nuring him, he would have been protected by my immune system and could have come with me. The separation was ghastly for us both.

It's taken me many years and three babies to find out what my instincts could have told me from the start about breastfeeding and the bond it creates between mother and child. We've come a long way, baby, but civilization has dealt us a few rotten blows along the way. Gradually we are working our way back to nature.

A book like this is invaluable. More and more women are deciding to follow their instincts and nurse their babies. More and more new mothers return to work refusing to give up the special closeness and comfort that nursing gives them and their newborns.

Lynn Redgrave

Introduction

Today, over 50 percent of all women with preschool-age children are employed outside the home. That percentage has doubled over the last ten years. And half of all new mothers return to work within one year, an increase of 26 percent since 1980.

Over 60 percent of these employed mothers breastfeed their babies at birth, which is comparable to the number of nonemployed mothers who breastfeed. But after five or six months, fewer than 20 percent of employed mothers continue breastfeeding.

Why do so many women stop breastfeeding after the first few months? For the working mother, it's usually her return to work that makes her give up breastfeeding, as she becomes frustrated with juggling motherhood and employment 24 hours a day. But this doesn't have to happen. It is possible to achieve a balance between motherhood and employment and to continue breastfeeding for as long as you want.

That's the goal of this book: to help you achieve this balance and learn how to manage being an employed, breastfeeding mother. We will begin by discussing the advantages breastfeeding offers—to the mother, the baby, and even the employer. We will also provide the technical information necessary to breastfeed successfully, including the basics of nursing, pumping and storing milk, and selecting a breast pump. In later chapters, we will address the preparations necessary for both the mother and the baby, such as negotiating a maternity leave and choosing the right daycare situation. And finally, we will review various work arrangements and the choices that mothers now have.

In addition to this information, we provide examples of real-life mothers and how they've managed motherhood and employment. And we offer our own experience here, too. For as La Leche League leaders, we helped countless mothers. And we have both been employed, breastfeeding mothers ourselves, so we are speaking from experience.

Based on that experience, we offer our help. Because if you want to nurse your baby while you are employed, we strongly feel that you deserve the support that will make it work.

Anne Price
Nancy Dana

Chapter 1

Why Breastfeed?

Why would anyone want to breastfeed **and** work? Good question!

Women choose to breastfeed when they realize the advantages it provides for both mother and child. In this chapter, we will discuss some of the most obvious advantages of breastfeeding, including health and emotional factors. We will also discuss many of the advantages that apply to the special circumstances of the employed mother. As you read this chapter, you may realize other advantages that relate to your own situation, some of which may be the most meaningful of all.

Health

Breastfed babies are physically healthier than bottlefed babies. Breastfed babies experience only one-seventh the infections that affect their bottlefed counterparts. Of course, this does not mean that your particular breastfed baby will definitely be healthier than your neighbor's bottlefed baby. But when the two groups are compared statistically, breastfed babies are sick far less often than bottlefed babies.

Breastfed babies are less prone to infection for several reasons:

1. A breastfed baby receives antibodies from his mother's colostrum and later from her milk. Colostrum is the premilk fluid present in the mother's breasts during late pregnancy and the first postpartum days. It is a thick, yellow liquid, designed specifically for an infant's early days. It is higher in protein and calories than breast milk; it helps clear mucus from the baby's throat; and its laxative effect helps clear out the stool that accumulates in *utero* (called *meconium*).

But perhaps the most important benefit of colostrum is its immunological effect. Colostrum passes the mother's antibodies on to the baby, which protects the child from disease. Moreover, recent research indicates that this immunological protection does not diminish with time, as was once thought. In

1

fact, high levels of antibodies are present throughout the first year of lactation and are maintained through the second year, as well.

2. A breastfed baby is less likely to have intestinal infections. Breast milk creates an acidic environment in the baby's intestines, which discourages bacterial growth. As long as the baby ingests nothing but breast milk, he receives this protection.

The lower rate of diarrhea in breastfed babies can be attributed in part to the predominance of bifidobacteria in relation to enterobacteria in the baby's system, as determined by stool samples. In a six-day-old breastfed baby, the ratio of bifidobacteria to enterobacteria was 1,000 to 1. In formula-fed babies, enterobacteria dominates. In a six-day-old formula-fed baby, the ratio of enterobacteria to bifidobacteria was 10 to 1. By the age of one month, bifidobacteria was predominant in both groups of babies. But in bottlefed babies, the number of these helpful organisms was only one-tenth the amount found in breastfed babies.

3. Ear infections are less common in breastfed babies, as well. In a 1982 study, 28 percent of the babies breastfed for six months or longer experienced ear infections during their first year of life, compared to 53 percent of the babies breastfed for two months or less.

Although we don't know for sure why the incidence of ear infection is so much lower for breastfed babies, one factor may be the position in which the baby feeds. When a baby drinks from a bottle while lying on his back, the pressure that results from the sucking can cause milk to enter the middle ear, leading to an ear infection. But when a baby is breastfed, this is not a problem, for two reasons: (a) Sucking at the breast does not cause the same type of pressure that sucking on a bottle does; and (b) the child is held more upright while nursed than while bottlefed.

Certainly, every mother wants to have a healthy baby for the baby's sake. But having a healthy baby also makes Mom's life easier. It simplifies her day-to-day physical activities and eases the emotional pressures she feels.

This is especially important to the employed mother. For when her child is sick, she not only has to deal with the normal parental anxieties. She also has to deal with special work-related circumstances. For instance, the babysitter will probably not want to care for a sick baby, which means that someone has to stay home with the child. Unless you are a single parent, it may be possible for you and your partner to alternate days at home. Unfortunately, not all work situations are that flexible. And it's impossible to predict the timing or duration of your baby's illness. What if you have an important meeting to attend or have to travel? Even if you can go to work, you'll be up more at night with a sick baby, which will make your work day that much harder. And so it seems that there is no good solution. You'll either be at work, worrying about your baby, or at home, worrying about your work!

Having a healthy baby makes the employed mother's life much easier. It frees her from the extra work and strain that go along with having a sick child. And in doing so, it gives her the flexibility and energy to be both a good mother and a good worker.

Nutrition

The most obvious advantage of breastfeeding is nutrition. Breast milk is nutritionally perfect. Human milk has evolved over millions of years to become the perfect food for the development of human babies. Milk from another species simply cannot compare.

Breast milk contains about half the protein of cow's milk, which makes it appropriate for the rate of human muscle growth, and slightly more fat, making calcium more available for the growth of bones and teeth. In addition, breast milk contains a greater amount of the primary carbohydrate found in cow's milk, lactose, which provides energy and discourages bacteria growth. Breast milk also contains more water and less salt than cow's milk and provides the perfect proportions of minerals, vitamins, and iron for the development and growth of the human baby.

Another important nutritional consideration is allergies. Research shows that breastfeeding for at least the first three months of life—thus avoiding common food and environmental allergens—probably plays an important role in preventing allergies in childhood and adolescence. According to Robert Mendelsohn, M.D., bottlefed babies are "at least twenty times" more likely to develop allergies than breastfed babies.

Breastfed babies are less prone to developing allergies for several reasons:

1. Breastfed babies ingest colostrum, which performs a task called *gut closure*. When a baby is born, the large intestine is somewhat permeable; as a result, whole proteins (from food or formula) can pass undigested through the intestinal wall. When this happens, the baby's body produces antibodies to the substance, causing an allergy. However, when a baby ingests colostrum through breast milk, gut closure greatly reduces intestinal permeability. Whole proteins thus remain within the large intestine to be properly digested, and no allergy results.

2. Breastfed babies are not exposed to cow's milk, which is an extremely common allergen during the first twelve months. The protein in cow's milk and formula can sometimes cause problems for the human infant. A fairly high percentage of babies exposed to these foreign proteins become sensitized. About 20 percent of these allergic babies outgrow their cow's milk allergy by the age of twelve months, when their digestive system is more mature.

Although it is impossible for a baby to be allergic to his own mother's milk, it is possible for a very sensitive baby to react to something ingested by the mother and passed to the child through her milk. The most common offenders are dairy products, gas-producing vegetables (such as broccoli and cauliflower), iron supplements, and large amounts of carbonated beverages, caffeine, and nicotine.

Another consideration that is particularly important to the employed mother of an allergic baby is daycare. It is always difficult for parents to work with the special dietary needs of an allergic child. But asking a daycare center or babysitter to accommodate these needs is even more difficult. Again, breastfeeding may prevent you from having to deal with allergies altogether.

Bear in mind that very few babies are so sensitive. If your baby does have a fussy period, it is probably not related to your diet. Also remember that a food sensitivity is not an allergy. Even adults react differently to different foods.

Bonding and Emotional Security

Bonding is the attachment process that takes place between newborns and their parents. You feel overwhelmingly attached to and "in love with" your baby. The future of your relationship with your child is related to the quality of the bond you form with him during infancy.

Although early nursing may seem insignificant because of the small amount of nourishment the baby actually takes from the breast, it serves an important role in bonding. Breastfeeding is the perfect way of providing the two main elements of bonding: eye contact and physical closeness.

The newborn is biologically geared to look for the human face and can focus best on an object ten to fifteen inches away. Perhaps not so coincidentally, when a baby is at the breast, that is usually the distance from the child's eyes to the mother's face. You will probably find that, as you nurse, your baby will stare intently at your face. And you will undoubtedly find yourself gazing back in love and amazement. Mother and child are much like young lovers— they can stare into each other's eyes for hours!

The second element of bonding—physical closeness—is also provided by breastfeeding. As you hold your baby close to your body while nursing, you experience direct, skin-to-skin contact. In fact, you will find yourself instinctively touching and stroking your child all over. And since a new baby nurses frequently, breastfeeding supplies the large amounts of close contact time that both you and the baby need.

We aren't suggesting that a bottlefeeding mother will not experience the eye contact and physical closeness that are part of bonding. But breastfeeding

Breastfeeding can play an important role in how you and your baby create a loving and lasting bond.

provides the perfect components of bonding. It would seem impossible not to bond while breastfeeding.

In addition to the initial mother-child attachment that is formed, breastfeeding also contributes to the child's emotional security and happiness. The simple continuity provided by breastfeeding helps build the security we all hope our children will have.

Some people feel that breastfed babies are more spoiled and demanding than bottlefed babies. This conclusion is certainly not true, but we can trace the thought behind it. Breastfeeding mothers are very tuned-in and responsive to their babies' needs, due in part to the extra skin-to-skin contact and the mother's hormonal state. (See the section "Hormonal Benefits," p. 8.)

They communicate this to their child: "You can trust me. I believe your needs are legitimate and you can make them known to me. You can count on me to satisfy them." When a child feels this security, he will feel loved enough to express his needs. Moreover, an important emotional foundation is provided as the child learns to trust and develop true emotional security.

The extended contact between you and your baby is a loving experience and a very special element in your relationship. Be sure to share these feelings with your partner, too. Obviously, he cannot nurse the baby, but he can be involved in other loving and touching activities. For instance, bathing the baby is a perfect way for a father to have skin-to-skin contact with his child; once the baby is a little older, showering together can be fun, too. And Dad can always enjoy cuddling and rocking the baby. However it is accomplished, the father should be encouraged and helped to be physically close to his child. Experiencing the joys of parenthood is important to the development of the father-child relationship.

You may also find that this sharing contributes to your overall family relationship, as well. Having the baby sleep with you is an easy way for the whole family to experience a physical closeness that is good for everyone's well-being. Some families may not be comfortable sleeping with their baby, and

Fathers should be encouraged to get close to their babies. Experiencing the joys of parenthood is important to the development of the father-child relationship.

that's fine. However, you shouldn't worry about hurting the child. There is no evidence to suggest that this is a realistic worry.

Benefits to the Mother
Convenience

In addition to the physical and emotional benefits that result from breastfeeding is the simple pleasure of convenience. In fact, when asked about what they value most about breastfeeding, most mothers rank ease and convenience at or near the top of their list. They appreciate not having to prepare formula, wash bottles and nipples, and heat up milk before feeding the baby.

An added plus of this convenience is psychological. It is wonderful to be able to sit down and relax while nursing your baby, without having to face the ordeal of preparing a bottle while jiggling a tired, impatient child on your hip.

The time and energy saved by breastfeeding also contribute to your emotional state. Feeling good about your baby's well-being and enjoying the special relationship between you and your child will make you feel secure about motherhood and life in general.

Of course, this convenience is diminished somewhat when you go back to work and begin pumping and toting bottles to the babysitter. But expressing breast milk is not an insurmountable problem, as we will discuss in Chapter 5. Just keep in mind that you will still be able to enjoy the convenience of nursing when you're at home.

In fact, the employed mother will appreciate the convenience of breastfeeding even more. When she gets home from work, she is most likely too tired to move. She would like to be able to sit down, relax, and enjoy being home with her family. The last thing she needs is to have to prepare formula and heat bottles.

Nursing provides a welcome alternative. It makes life easier and saves time that can be used for other activities. And time is a precious commodity for an employed mother, who is, by definition, a very busy person.

Financial Savings

Breastfeeding saves a lot of money. It costs approximately $1.50 a day to formula-feed a baby; over six months, this adds up to almost $300. Breastfeeding, on the other hand, is free. Even if a mother pumps and stores breast milk, the cost of a breast pump and bottles is still much less than that of buying formula.

You may have heard that a mother must eat more when breastfeeding, which would mean spending more on her own food. This is of concern only if you are very thin and wish to avoid the gradual, natural weight loss that occurs during breastfeeding. Most women are delighted to lose their weight and simply eat to satisfy their hunger.

If you do find yourself hungrier than usual—and you may—an inexpensive caloric boost like a peanut butter sandwich and a glass of milk is all you need. And this is still less than the cost of formula!

Hormonal Benefits

No one will argue with the fact that early motherhood can be very trying. But again, nature's plan is evident.

Normally, a woman's dominant hormones are estrogen and progesterone, which regulate her menstrual cycle. But when a woman is breastfeeding, her dominant hormones are oxytocin and prolactin.

Oxytocin is called "nature's tranquilizer," and it lives up to that name. At one time or another, most nursing women have observed that, no matter how harried and hassled they may feel, once they settle down and begin to nurse, a wonderful, relaxing sensation comes over them. This is the effect of oxytocin. During these demanding and trying years of motherhood, it seems only fair that Nature provides us with a continually refillable prescription for a free, natural, and safe tranquilizer!

The second dominant hormone, prolactin, is sometimes called "the mothering hormone." It creates powerful maternal feelings that make you feel close to your baby. Actually, these feelings are so strong that you may feel uneasy when away from your child.

You will miss your baby while you are at work, and you may hold him all the more when you are home. But you will adjust to your new lifestyle as an employed, nursing mother. In fact, the sense of attachment that is enhanced by prolactin may be especially healthy for the employed mother and her baby because it makes their relationship more exclusive and intimate.

Reproductive System

Breastfeeding contributes to the mother's health in several ways:

1. As discussed earlier, when a mother nurses, oxytocin becomes one of the dominant hormones in her system. In addition to having a tranquilizing effect, oxytocin also triggers uterine contractions. Nursing immediately after birth, while still on the delivery table, will help expel the placenta. And in the weeks following delivery, the contractions brought on by oxytocin will prevent hemorrhage and help return your uterus to its original prepregnancy size and shape. Because of this effect, some hospitals allow breastfeeding mothers to be discharged only hours after they give birth.

2. Breastfeeding will delay a mother's menstrual period. Again, a woman's hormonal balance changes while breastfeeding. More specifically, frequent nipple stimulation maintains dominance of the hormones prolactin and oxytocin and suppresses the hormones estrogen and progesterone. Since estrogen and progesterone regulate the menstrual cycle, when they are suppressed, a woman does not have a period. Any prolonged decrease in nursing, such as that which occurs when the baby starts eating solids or sleeping through the night, could cause your hormonal balance to change, thus causing your period. This could also happen when you return to work and begin pumping.

A related topic in our discussion of the nursing mother's reproductive system is that of birth control. Chances are slim that a nursing mother will become pregnant without having had a period first. Remember, though, that **just because you do not menstruate does not mean that you cannot become pregnant.** In this sense, breastfeeding is not a reliable method of birth control!

Recommended birth control measures for the breastfeeding woman include the diaphragm, cervical cap, condom, vaginal suppository or sponge, and spermicidal cream, foam, and jelly. The hormones in birth control pills and hormone-coated IUDs make them unadvisable for breastfeeding women; many health professionals even frown on the use of the lower-dose "minipill" during lactation. And although many breastfeeding women have used uncoated IUDs successfully, the risk of perforating the uterus is greater during breastfeeding because of the uterine cramping that naturally occurs. You should discuss birth control pills and IUDs carefully with your health professional before using either.

If you intend to incorporate breastfeeding as a part of your family planning, refer to *Breastfeeding and Natural Child Spacing: The Ecology of Natural Mothering,* by Sheila Kipley (Penguin Books, 1975).

Weight Loss

During pregnancy, your body stores calcium, fat, and nutrients, which you will need during lactation. If you nurse, your baby uses up these stored supplies. Consequently, you lose weight. It is estimated that a woman burns between 500 and 1,000 calories a day breastfeeding, depending on the age of the baby and how much milk he is taking.

This weight loss may be especially appreciated by employed mothers, who want to return to work wearing normal clothes and looking trim. Be aware, however, that the weight loss during nursing is slow and gradual; it does not happen overnight.

Some women find that they lose a large amount of weight immediately after birth and then experience a slow but steady loss. Others have a weight-loss pattern of sudden drops and plateaus. If you are anxious about not losing weight quickly enough, stay away from desserts and nonnutritious snacks. But don't forget that your appetite will probably be very good and your energy needs high, so be sensible about your weight loss. Your body will require plenty of good nourishment to handle the demands of being a working, nursing mother. During this time, your health and well-being should take precedence over your desire to be thin.

Advantages to the Employer

The advantages of breastfeeding are not limited to just mother and baby. They extend to the mother's employer and even her co-workers.

1. Nursing mothers will seldom miss work because their babies are sick. As we discussed at the beginning of the chapter, breastfed babies experience a small fraction of the infections and allergies that affect bottlefed babies. Breastfeeding mothers will therefore spend less time at home with sick children. Co-workers, as well as employers, appreciate this regularity.

2. Nursing mothers may be healthier themselves, too. Since she is providing nourishment for her baby, a breastfeeding woman is very nutrition-conscious—certainly more than she would be otherwise. And since breastfeeding is more convenient than bottlefeeding, the nursing mother has more time to relax and enjoy her off hours. She will not feel as run down and hassled as a mother who also has to include preparing bottles of formula in her already overloaded life. As a result, she will be more pleasant to work with and more competent and efficient in performing her job.

3. If the employer is actively supportive of the employed mother—as some are—they will receive back the benefit of the employee's goodwill. The employer will also enjoy lower employee turnover rates, which is a considerable financial savings.

When you look at the number of employed mothers in the workforce today, these employer advantages become a significant concern. Consider the following example.

PCA International, Inc., a processor of color portraits with 3,000 employees, has instituted a policy allowing nursing mothers to take breastfeeding breaks. The company provides an on-site daycare center, and a child care staff member calls the employee when her baby is ready to nurse. Joan Narron, director of the child care center, says that the program has brought the company more advantages than disadvantages. For instance, the company's policy supporting and aiding the breastfeeding mothers has helped PCA keep valued employees. In addition, mothers have returned to work earlier than they might have had the company not sponsored breastfeeding breaks and child care.

"Employees don't take advantage," Narron points out. On the contrary, she says that most of the women try to compensate for any lost time by cutting their scheduled breaks short. Employees at PCA felt that the opportunity to continue breastfeeding contributed to their babies' good health, which helped them miss less work.

Another successful yet different example of an employer's support of breastfeeding is seen in Fisher and Associates, a rehabilitation firm. Owner Donna Ferris allows an employee to bring her nursing infant to work with her each day. According to Donna, the baby is not at all disruptive and the mother still performs her job well. There is also an added plus to this arrangement: The staff is delighted to be involved with their co-worker's baby. "We're all aunts and uncles now," Donna adds.

Both of these examples demonstrate that employers receive benefits when they support nursing workers and mothers in general. Certainly, some of these benefits—like employee attitude and office environment—may seem somewhat intangible and difficult to measure. But they all contribute to making workers more stable, happy, and productive. And this provides the employer with very tangible financial benefits.

Summary

So, why bother breastfeeding? Because breastfeeding offers important advantages for the child, mother, and employer.

For the child, breastfeeding provides two primary advantages:

• better physical health, due to protection from infection and receiving perfect nutrition; and

• better emotional health, since nursing supports bonding and the development of long-lasting feelings of love and security.

For the mother, breastfeeding provides many important benefits:

• convenience—both practical and psychological—since nursing requires no special preparation and thus additional effort;

• financial savings—it's free;

• better physical health, including improved eating habits and progressive weight loss; and

• better emotional health, due to the close mother-child attachment that is formed and the peace of mind that comes from knowing that your child is healthy and secure.

Breastfeeding also offers benefits for the employer:

• better employee health, because nursing mothers are conscious of their own health;

• better employee attitude and thus productivity, particularly if the employer is supportive of employed mothers;

• less absenteeism by mothers with sick children; and

• lower employee turnover rates, again, particularly if the employer is supportive.

There is no doubt, then, that breastfeeding provides many benefits to mother, child, and employer. But it is still difficult for a woman to be both a worker and a mother, let alone a nursing mother!

When you find yourself dwelling on the difficulties, consider how breastfeeding makes life easier and happier. In her book *Nursing Your Baby*, Karen Pryor offers this encouragement to mothers who are employed and breastfeeding:

When the baby is nine or ten months old or older, it is almost easier to work or finish school if the baby is nursing than if he is not. The closeness of the nursing relationship, the reassurance of the breast when you come home each day, make your absences easier for the baby to tolerate, and makes him a cheerier, less demanding baby when you come home.

No matter what the baby's age, the mother who works and nurses should really be proud of herself. She is working extra hard and doing the best she can for her child.

And for herself, too!

Chapter 2

Basics:
The Right Start
Can Make it Work

Since breastfeeding is the natural way for a mother to feed her child, many people assume that knowing how to nurse is completely instinctive. While the feelings of mothering and nurturing may be, the basic techniques of nursing are not. Breastfeeding is something that you must learn.

Most women do experience some difficulty learning to nurse; this can be demoralizing, particularly for the first-time mother. But don't feel defeated if you aren't a nursing expert immediately. None of us were! Everyone goes through that period where Mother and Baby are trying to figure out exactly how to nurse. If you are as informed as possible before you start and know you may need a little help, you will be less likely to quit in frustration. Persevere through the learning stage, and you and your baby will reap the many rewards of nursing.

How the Breast Works

Before you learn how to do anything, it helps to know what it involves and how it all works. Knowing how the breast works will help you understand and avoid problems with breastfeeding and pumping your breasts.

First, a little general biology. Deep within the breast are grapelike clusters of milk-producing cells called *alveoli*. Surrounding each alveolus is a netlike cell—the *myoepithelial cell*—that contracts, causing the milk to flow from the alveoli into small channels called *lactiferous ducts*.

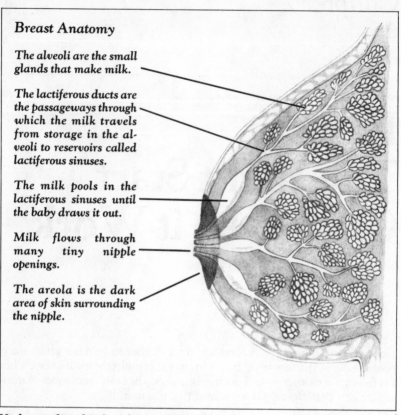

Breast Anatomy

The alveoli are the small glands that make milk.

The lactiferous ducts are the passageways through which the milk travels from storage in the alveoli to reservoirs called lactiferous sinuses.

The milk pools in the lactiferous sinuses until the baby draws it out.

Milk flows through many tiny nipple openings.

The areola is the dark area of skin surrounding the nipple.

Understanding the physiology and anatomy of the breast will increase your confidence in your ability to breastfeed.

The network of lactiferous ducts within the breast can be compared to a river system, where small streams—tributaries—merge as they travel, forming larger rivers. In the breast, these "tributaries" begin at the alveoli and lead to reservoirs called the *lactiferous sinuses*, which are just behind the *areola* (the brownish area surrounding the nipple).

When the baby sucks, she stimulates nerves in the nipple, which sends a message to the pituitary gland in the brain. This signals the release of two hormones: prolactin and oxytocin. *Prolactin* causes the milk to be secreted, and *oxytocin* activates the myoepithelial cells surrounding the alveoli, causing them to snap down and literally squeeze the milk from the alveoli into the lactiferous ducts. The milk then moves through the ducts and collects in the lactiferous sinuses. This is called the *letdown reflex*.

Most mothers find the letdown sensation quite pleasant, since it evokes very motherly and nurturing feelings.

When this reflex occurs, many women feel a tingling or a mild ache. Although it may sound uncomfortable to a woman who has not nursed, most mothers find the letdown sensation quite pleasant, since it evokes very motherly and nurturing feelings.

In the first days of breastfeeding, some women do not feel the letdown sensation. Likewise, as the baby grows out of infancy, some mothers lose the sensation again.

It is important to separate the **sensation** from the **function.** It is rare for a woman not to **have** a letdown reflex, but it is not rare for a woman not to **feel** a letdown. On the other hand, if the letdown reflex is very strong, a woman may have problems with milk leaking or even spraying out of her nipples.

Once the mother is ready to nurse, how does the baby get milk out of the breast? As explained above, the baby's sucking provides the initial stimulation for the mother. However, the child doesn't simply suck the milk out. She uses her tongue to draw the nipple back into her mouth and holds it there by using negative pressure, or suction. She actually extracts the milk by pumping with her jaws.

The Basic How-To

Our discussion here will provide you with the basics of breastfeeding—the general background information necessary for successful nursing. We will also comment on relevant work-related issues. Should you want to explore this subject more thoroughly, consult our general breastfeeding book, *Successful Breastfeeding* (Meadowbrook, Inc., 1985).

Nipple Preparation

You may have heard that you should rub your nipples with a towel to toughen them up or pull at them to make the nipples more pliable. Indeed, we used to recommend these measures to nursing mothers. However, new research indicates that neither measure is really helpful.

These rubbing and pulling techniques were intended to condition the nipple for nursing and thus reduce the chance of soreness. We know now that the best way to prevent nipple soreness is to learn and employ proper positioning of the baby at the breast for every nursing from the start. Rather than prepare your nipples, you must learn proper positioning. (See "Positioning the Baby," pp. 17-21.)

Once your baby is nursing, follow these measures to prevent soreness:

• After a nursing, air dry your nipples. Do not rub them dry using a cloth or towel.

• Never put on your bra while your nipples are still wet, and never put on a wet bra. Always keep your nipples as dry as possible.

• Keep extra nursing pads with you at work. If your bra becomes wet, you can at least keep a dry pad next to your nipples.

• Once your nipples are dry, try applying a thin coat of a moisturizer like A&D Ointment or hydrous lanolin, which is a pure lanolin product available without a prescription at many pharmacies. This will be especially helpful in the early weeks; most women discontinue using ointments after that. Remember, though, to wipe off as much of the excess ointment as you can before nursing so the baby doesn't ingest it.

Timing

Some hospitals recommend that you nurse for a restricted number of minutes on each breast the first day and gradually increase. But not everyone agrees that this sort of conditioning helps prevent soreness. To start with one minute a day and build up is very restrictive. Yet totally unlimited nursing may be too much at first.

Since there are contradicting theories on how timing affects nipple soreness, we recommend the moderate path: Nurse about five minutes on each side at each nursing the first day, ten minutes the second day, and fifteen the third day. After that, nurse for an unlimited amount of time at each nursing. Do be flexible, though. Some babies don't really settle into nursing for just five minutes.

In general, you don't need to worry much about timing your nursings, even in the beginning. The amount of time you nurse is rarely the cause of sore nipples. If you do get sore nipples from excessive nursing, you might have gotten them from limited nursing, too, only a few days later.

Should you get sore nipples despite following preventive measures, see our discussion of treatments later in this chapter (p. 26).

Nursing Positions

When you always nurse in the same position, the point of stress on the nipple remains the same, which can cause soreness. Changing positions changes the areas that receive pressure and decreases your chance of soreness.

Alternate nursing positions frequently. For instance, sit up for one nursing, and lie down for the next. Lying down to nurse may feel awkward at first, until you discover the most comfortable position, but it can be wonderfully relaxing once you learn to do it. This may be especially relaxing for the working mother who's been active all day.

Positioning the Baby

Positioning the baby properly at the breast is the single most important factor in preventing nipple soreness and nursing efficiently. This point is illustrated clearly by the following example.

One Colorado mother, Jan, nursed her first baby, Dana, for about two months, during which time the baby gained very little weight. Jan also commented on having very sore nipples during these two months. After attending a La Leche League meeting and hearing the correct nursing position described, Jan discovered what her problem had been: She had been allowing her baby to nurse on her nipples alone, rather than teaching her to pull some

Nursing Positions

Alternate nursing positions frequently, sitting up for one nursing and lying down for the next.

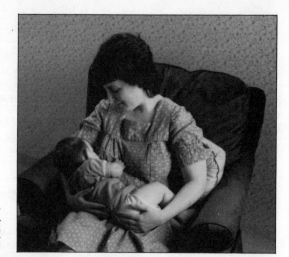

of the areola into her mouth. And because the baby was sucking only on the nipple, she did not open her mouth very much. As a result, Dana was unable to get any great quantities of milk from her mother's breasts, since she was not pumping the lactiferous sinuses. She was probably only receiving the milk that came out with the letdown reflex. This milk is high in nutrients and protein but very low in fat, which explains Dana's slow weight gain. Jan also realized that her soreness was caused by the continual pressure being exerted directly on her nipples.

Kittie Frantz, director of the Breastfeeding Infant Clinic at the Los Angeles County/University of Southern California Medical Center and a La Leche League leader, developed the following guidelines for getting the baby onto the breast correctly. This information is crucial for successful nursing, so make sure you understand each step.

Proper Positioning at the Breast

1. Place the side (not the back) of the baby's head in the crook of your arm as you settle in to nurse. Bring the arm that's holding the baby around her back and hold on to her top thigh or buttocks, with your palm facing toward you. You need to hold the baby securely in order to be able to control her position; then pull her bottom up, toward you.

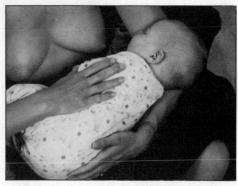

Make sure the baby's whole body is facing yours so you are face to breast, abdomen to abdomen, knees to belly, and so forth.

2. Hold your breast with your free hand. Place **all** of your fingers under the breast and your thumb on top of the breast, behind the areola.

This position allows you to support your breast for the entire feeding, if need be. This is sometimes necessary with a tiny infant, especially if you have large breasts; if she has to use all her strength to hold your breast in her mouth, she won't have much left for good sucking.

This hand position also keeps your fingers behind the areola, so they won't interfere with the area the baby needs to take into her mouth. This is the disadvantage of the scissors position, which is commonly used.

Holding the breast this way also allows you to move your nipple up and down and to center it in the baby's mouth. If you push in with your thumb, your nipple will point up. If you push in with your fingers, it will point down. Try it—it moves! Pointing the nipple downward often makes it easier for the baby to take the breast properly.

3. Bring the baby up to your breast and tickle her upper lip gently with your nipple. Within a few moments, this should cause her to open her mouth wide. Be sure to tickle her lip **gently**—your baby won't respond to you forcing your nipple against her lips.

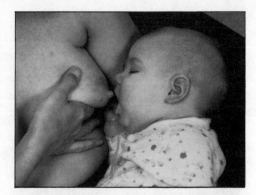

4. Once the baby's mouth is open very wide, center your nipple and pull the baby close. Don't pull her close if her mouth is not opened wide or if the nipple is not centered. Wait until everything is right.

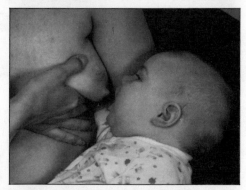

5. When the baby is nursing properly, her bottom lip will be curled out.

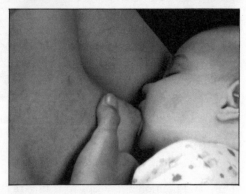

You may hear that your entire areola must be in the baby's mouth for her to be nursing correctly, but this is not always possible or necessary. Some women simply have larger areolas than others, so it is impossible to make a definitive rule on how much of the areola will go into the baby's mouth. Your nipple will reach to the back of the baby's mouth when she is nursing properly, which means that at least a great deal of your areola will go into her mouth.

If you follow this procedure, chances are very good that your baby will suck with great efficiency and that you will not have sore nipples. If you experience no discomfort, you can be fairly sure that the baby has the breast in her mouth properly and that your position is okay.

It may sound as if you must go to great lengths to engineer something that should be natural, but, in fact, you are simply overseeing the natural process. Your nursing technique will become habit very quickly, so it is wise to establish good habits from the start.

To obtain diagrams of this nursing procedure, contact the La Leche League and ask for reprint #11, "Managing Nipple Problems," by Kittie Frantz (RNC, PNP).

Getting the Baby On and Off the Breast

Nursing is something you must learn. So don't be frustrated at the start if the seemingly simple aspects of nursing loom large when you are faced with them for the first time.

Remember, if the baby does not open her mouth wide enough, take her off and put her on again until she is on the breast correctly. Don't let your baby get used to nursing in an incorrect position, even for a short time. Doing so can lead to sucking problems and slow weight gain. Most babies adopt the proper position quite naturally. If your child doesn't, work with her in the beginning, and before you know it, her positioning will become both proper and comfortable.

To get the baby off the breast, you can wait until she falls asleep or lets go. If you want to take the baby off or switch sides while she is still sucking, slip your finger into her mouth to break the suction and then take her off. Never just pull the baby off. It will hurt! We heard of one woman who only discovered this painless way of getting the baby off the breast while nursing her fifth baby!

Supply and Demand

In the days right after your baby is born, your breasts will contain colostrum, which provides important nourishment for the baby, as discussed in the last chapter. Within a few days, your milk will "come in," and you will probably have more than your baby needs at that point.

During these early days, you may feel engorged or overly full. You may even leak. This is due to the supply-and-demand nature of lactation. Your body starts out producing in excess and then cuts back to meet the actual demand. But in the beginning, your body has no demand by which to regulate supply.

You see, the milk-making mechanism can be compared to a computer. The baby "programs" the computer by taking out the amount of milk she needs, thus relieving a certain amount of pressure from within the breast. It is believed that the breast takes its information on milk production from this pressure. In other words, the less milk that is emptied, the less milk the breast is programmed to produce. The more often and more thoroughly the breast is emptied, the more milk the breast will produce.

For this reason, it is important to get the baby to nurse on both sides each time. Both breasts need stimulation and emptying to keep producing milk. Keep in mind, though, that some babies insist on nursing on just one side at each feeding. These babies seem to empty that one side more thoroughly and generally do fine. It is still better for your supply, though, for your baby to nurse on both sides at each nursing, if she will.

Fat and Nutrient Content

The makeup of breast milk changes over the course of a single feeding. When you begin nursing, you are giving the baby what is called *fore milk*. This milk lasts for about the first third of a feeding. It is thin and watery and contains little fat and few calories. It does, however, contain most of the nutrients.

For the rest of the feeding, you are giving the baby *hind milk*. It contains a high percentage of fat and has a high calorie content, but it is low in nutrients.

Obviously, it is essential that the baby gets both the fore and hind milk in order to grow properly. A short nursing could result in less hind milk for the baby. This is another reason for not severely limiting the baby's time at the breast. It is difficult to say how long it takes a baby to "empty" the breast. When she is no longer swallowing (but has been—audibly), she probably has taken all of the milk from that breast.

"Saving" Milk

You may hear that, to increase her milk supply, a mother should nurse less often and thus "save" her milk. This is nothing but a misconception. By heeding this bad advice, many women have diminished their milk supply to the point of being completely unable to nourish their babies. Follow the rule of supply and demand: If you cut back the demand, your body will reduce the supply.

Growth Spurts

Often, a few days after birth and at six weeks, three months, and six months, your baby will experience a growth spurt. Most likely, she will need more milk than she has been taking.

The clear remedy is to nurse more often, perhaps every hour or two—or maybe even more in some cases—for a couple of days. By nursing this much, your baby's increased hunger will be satisfied, and she will "reprogram the computer" at the same time, since your milk supply will keep up with this new demand. Then, once your baby is through her spurt, you can both return to a normal feeding schedule.

Growth spurts are not a problem if you follow this natural supply-and-demand process, which works for both you and your baby. But some mothers interfere with this process by feeding the baby a formula supplement, which begins a cycle that is hard to break. If you satisfy the baby's hunger by giving her formula, she will have less desire to suckle at the breast. Less sucking means less milk, which means more supplement—and so goes the cycle. It is far better to work through a few taxing days of extra nursing and to build up an adequate supply again the natural way.

Growth spurts can be especially difficult for the employed mother. If your milk supply is much too low for your baby's demand, a day or two home from work (if at all possible) may be the best solution. Just take the baby into bed with you and nurse and rest around the clock. You'll build up your supply and your energy, too.

If a day at home is not possible, at least spend all of a couple of evenings and nights in bed together with your baby. The combination of extra rest and extra nursing will go far to boost your milk supply.

Nursing Frequency

How often should you nurse your baby? Generally, it is best to let your baby set her own schedule, since she alone knows when she is hungry. This is called *demand feeding*.

An obvious exception to this rule is the placid new baby who goes for long periods without feeding or sleeps through the night. It is not a good idea to let new babies go more than three or four hours between nursings, and they should nurse at least once during the night. Most new babies will nurse about every two or three hours, around the clock. These times will probably get farther apart as the baby gets older and is able to take more milk at each feeding.

One of the most common questions about nursing is: How soon after a single nursing will there be enough milk for the baby to nurse again? You can nurse as often as you and the baby want to, because your breasts are continually producing milk. If you feel your milk supply is down, nurse more and you will build it up. Although it probably takes about two hours before your supply is replenished, don't feel that you have to wait that long before nursing again. There will always be something there.

If you are back at work and pumping instead of nursing during much of the day, you will need to nurse during the night and on weekends and days off to keep up your supply. If you can keep this thought in mind during night nursings, they may seem like a real blessing. Many women find that, on the days they work, they must nurse at least four times in a twenty-four hour period to maintain an adequate supply. (This is usually in addition to the pumping they do at work.)

Getting Off to a Good Start
In the Hospital

As we discussed in Chapter 1 on the advantages of breastfeeding, the first few hours with your new baby are important to your bonding as a family. So during your first few hours together, take the time to get close to your baby. This is the perfect time for both mother and father to touch, kiss, examine, and admire their new baby. Don't worry about the hospital's careful "gift wrapping" of your baby. Getting close is what's important.

All babies respond differently to nursing, so be flexible. Some seem to be born with the knack and will latch on and suck easily right away. Some will have a great desire to suckle but will not be able to figure out how to do it. Others will merely nuzzle or lick at the breast, while some will seem too sleepy to even try.

To prepare yourself, review the "Positioning the Baby" section (pp. 17–21) of this chapter before you go to the hospital to become familiar with the procedure for getting the baby on and off the breast.

Since nursing stimulates hormones that help expel your placenta and contract your uterus to its prepregnancy size, it is very healthy to nurse shortly after birth. Even nuzzling at the breast can stimulate this hormonal release. But most of all, enjoy and extend these first moments immediately following birth.

Once you are settled in your room, nursing becomes nourishing as well as nurturing. This is the time to properly position the baby in order to start good habits. And this is the time to begin demand feeding: nursing the baby whenever she gets fussy or otherwise indicates that she wants to nurse. Let the baby set her own feeding schedule, unless she is going more than four hours between feedings.

Going Home

Try to make your time at home with your baby peaceful and restful for both of you. Once you go back to work, there will never again be enough hours in any day, so take advantage of the opportunity to rest and fully recuperate. If you rest enough during these early days, you will greatly reduce the possibility of depression ("baby blues") or illness later.

Your birth, hospital stay, and first days at home may range from being harried to helpful. Since so much stress is already inherent in having a baby, you should strive to alleviate as much additional stress as possible. Although you may have envisioned having lots of time to take care of things after the baby's birth and before you go back to work, this may not end up being true. Be prepared to spend your entire leave resting and caring for your baby. Then, if you feel well enough and your baby is cooperative enough, you can always do more.

Potential Difficulties

In this section, we will discuss a number of breastfeeding difficulties common among employed mothers. Be assured, though, that you will certainly not experience **all** of these problems. Most nursing mothers only have minor difficulties.

Engorgement

Your milk will come in anytime between the second and fifth day after birth. When it does come in, you may experience what is called *engorgement*, which is extreme fullness and tightness in your breasts, especially if it is your first baby. Some of this fullness is extra blood volume in your breast tissue, and some of it is milk.

You become engorged when your milk comes in because your baby has not yet "programmed" the milk-making mechanism within your breasts. You start out with too much milk because your breasts don't know how much your baby needs yet.

Engorgement usually goes away in a few days, after your baby has nursed and sent the correct supply messages. But you may continue to get very full and leak before each nursing for several weeks. You may also experience periodic engorgement to a lesser degree when you go back to work and begin to nurse less and pump more. Engorgement will be less of a problem if you try not to limit your baby's nursing time. Nurse as often and long as your baby likes.

During a period of engorgement, you may need to express or pump some milk before your baby begins to nurse. (See Chapter 5, "Hand Expression," pp. 80–87.) Relieving some of the fullness in the areola will make it easier for your baby to latch on and nurse. Express only enough to relieve the overfullness. This tactic will also be helpful in the early days of pumping if you find your breasts are too large to fit well into the flange of your pump.

Engorgement can also lead to sore nipples if you don't take any preventive steps. One mother told us:

I was incredibly engorged during the first couple weeks of Evan's life. My breasts were just huge and hard as rocks. I was really shocked by their condition. Poor Evan! He would be hungry and try to nurse, but since my breasts were so large and hard, he could get very little but my nipple into his mouth. Naturally, I really got sore. I didn't get better until I started expressing a little milk by hand before I nursed him so he could get more into his mouth.

Sore Nipples

Another problem you might experience is sore nipples. In our discussion of how to prevent soreness, we pointed out that the baby's nursing position is often the cause of this problem. In fact, this is the first and foremost cause of nipple soreness.

If you feel sore, check to make sure you have the baby on your breast correctly; her mouth should be open wide and her bottom lip should be curled outward. Also try alternating nursing positions frequently, sitting down for some nursings and lying down for others.

Many women relieve soreness by simply air drying their nipples after each nursing. It may also help to apply a thin layer of A&D Ointment or hydrous lanolin. Note that if you are allergic to wool, you may be sensitive to lanolin, too, since it comes from sheep's wool. And all nursing mothers should avoid lotions that contain perfumes or alcohol; they will be more irritating than soothing.

There are also some types of "home remedies" that may help relieve nipple soreness. We know of one maternity nurse who claims to have helped many new mothers recover from sore nipples by treating them with unscented Chap Stick. This treatment does make sense, since the skin of your nipples is much like that on your lips. And some hospitals recommend putting damp tea bags on your nipples; the tannic acid seems to be soothing. (Be careful—the tea can stain your bra or nightgown.) Plain old ice packs will also help relieve pain.

If you treat your nipples with any type of product, be sure to wipe off the excess before nursing your baby. But never wash your nipples with soap or alcohol. Just letting the water wash over them in the shower or bath is cleansing enough. Nature has provided small glands on your areola (Montgomery glands) to serve as cleansers. Again, the natural way is the best way.

Plugged Ducts and Breast Infection

The symptoms of a plugged duct or breast infection are easy to recognize: You will find a sore, inflamed, hard spot on your breast. The three general causes of this problem are restrictive clothing, exhaustion, and insufficient emptying. Since each of these factors can clearly be related to working, plugged ducts and possible infection is a common problem encountered by employed, breastfeeding mothers.

Pay attention to the fit of your bra. Make sure it is big enough for your new size. If you feel that it is binding or uncomfortably tight, change to a larger size.

Not all nursing women wear nursing bras to work. Some prefer simple, supportive cotton bras. Athletic bras are also a good choice. Avoid underwire bras.

A related hazard is exhausting yourself by strict dieting in a frantic effort to fit into your old work clothes again. Realize that your energy needs are greater than your fashion needs right now. Eat enough to feel good, and let the weight loss come gradually.

Insufficient emptying is probably the problem most likely to be faced by employed, breastfeeding mothers. Although you understand the importance of emptying your breasts when they become full, at times, your schedule may be too hectic to permit it. In addition to leaking and discomfort, the risk of a plugged duct is very real.

When your breasts feel full, try to pump them as soon as possible. If you don't have time for a real pumping, at least go into the restroom and express enough milk to relieve the fullness (even if you just hand express into the sink!).

If you do discover a plugged duct, do the following:

1. Apply heat to that spot. It will increase circulation and help clear the blocked area.

2. Nurse on the affected side first; keeping that side as empty as possible will relieve the pressure on the restricted duct. Again, it is helpful to vary positions. Gently massage the area in the direction toward the nipple while nursing.

3. Finally, try to get in some extra rest. Take a nap with the baby when you come home from work or on your days off.

If a plugged duct is discovered and treated immediately, it will probably not turn into a breast infection. But if it is not caught at this early stage, infection may result. If you have a breast infection, you will probably get a fever and feel generally fluish. You should consult your doctor, who will probably prescribe antibiotics. And follow the three treatment guidelines outlined above, as well.

A general note on medication: Taking antibiotics is not automatically prohibited during nursing. But you should always tell your doctor that you are nursing before you take any type of medication.

Actually, nursing is the most helpful thing you can do when you have a breast infection, since it is the easiest way to keep empty. Try to nurse more often so the affected side does not stay full.

A breast infection usually has no effect on the nursing baby. Occasionally, a very severe infection will cause a high bacteria count in the milk, and the baby will be taken off that side. This is rare, so don't assume that there's a problem with your milk unless your doctor tells you so. Continue to nurse as usual, offering the infected side first to keep it as empty as possible and promote healing. The breast infection should improve as soon as you begin to take the antibiotics.

Prevention is still the best cure, so be sure to get plenty of rest, especially if you are working, too. One working mother we talked to, Mary, was definitely able to link her breast infections to her exhaustion:

I was extremely prone to breast infections. It seemed like I had one after another. During the same period, my daughter, Sara, was competing in the "nonsleeper Olympics." Eventually, I noticed that an especially bad period of being up at night a great deal would be followed by a breast infection. I made a point to try to nap or rest after work during these periods. I also started taking large doses of vitamin C and I think that really helped.

Milk Supply

Most new breastfeeding mothers are concerned with their milk supply, because they can't see or measure the amount their baby receives. Eventually, though, they see wet diapers and a thriving baby and learn to trust the system.

Employed, breastfeeding mothers often worry about supply for the opposite reason: Since they pump milk, they can see whether they are up to their daily "production standard." The daily fuss of pumping can result in a mother being preoccupied with measurement to the point that even slight dips in the volume pumped may cause her to worry unnecessarily about her supply.

The concern with supply is somewhat legitimate in that, yes, it is a bit tougher to maintain a good supply when pumping for several feedings a day. Pumps are just not as effective as babies. But the issue is really magnified when pumping provides a daily quantification that other nursing mothers simply don't encounter.

Your milk supply will respond to the baby's demands. This is even true if your baby is bottlefed while you are at work and nursed while you are home. Mothers who follow this sort of routine—bottle by day, nursing by night— usually find that their supply adjusts, although it may take a little time. You won't feel as full during the day, but you will have plenty of milk at night when you normally nurse your baby.

We know a mother/magazine editor who used this alternating bottle/breast method. She told us, "My baby kept up night nursings and my supply stayed good during the hours I was home." Moreover, since she never gave her baby the bottle, the baby continued to expect only nursing from her mother. And since there was always milk, the baby's nursing was reinforced.

The amount of milk you produce is always a direct result of demand, so whether you are employed or not, it is normal to have supply ups and downs. But if you do have problems maintaining an adequate milk supply, try these strategies:

1. Make sure that you nurse exclusively during the time you are home. And nurse often and long. You don't have to wait for the baby to ask—you can offer to nurse. Also, don't underestimate the importance of night nursings. They may very well be the key to your nursing success. Spend long, lazy hours in bed nursing your baby on weekends. And if you can possibly manage it, take a day off now and then for R & R. Simply stay in bed and nurse as much as possible for the whole day.

2. If you find that you can't pump as many ounces as you once did, try pumping more often or consider renting an electric pump for a period of time. An electric pump will stimulate your supply more effectively than a manual pump will.

3. Control your rest and stress levels. This is the time to learn to say "no." Resist the urge to take on extra projects or bring work home if you don't absolutely have to. And don't work overtime if it can be avoided. At home, curb both excessive housework and socializing. Try going to bed earlier than usual for the first few months after the baby's birth. Rest as much as possible and give what energy you do have to the care of your new infant.

4. Maintain a healthy diet, too. Protein intake is related to milk production, so make an effort to include good sources of protein in your diet. Never substitute empty-calorie foods for nutritious ones. Keep nutritious snacks, like nuts and dried fruit, in places where you are likely to reach for them—in your car, on your desk, and at other convenient spots.

5. Also keep your fluid intake up. Nursing obviously uses some body fluids, and you don't want to become dehydrated. Your thirst will usually be a sufficient reminder to drink. However, don't be tempted to take most of your fluids from the office coffee pot or soda machine. Keep caffeine consumption moderate while you nurse. Bring a thermos of juice, herbal tea, mineral water, or whatever noncaffeinated drink you prefer to work with you.

If you still have problems with your milk supply, you can look into a product called a *nursing aid*. Quite simply, this device is a plastic bag that hangs around your neck. A tube runs from the bag down to your nipple. The baby nurses on your nipple, as usual, but she gets the supplement from the nursing aid in addition to what she gets from your breast. This neatly accomplishes two goals at once: (1) the baby receives more ounces per feeding and (2) nursing stimulates the mother's milk supply.

The nursing aid may be filled with thawed breast milk from your own frozen stockpile. But if you are having supply problems, you will probably have to use formula. Regardless, the purpose of the aid will be the same: Your baby will receive an adequate amount of food while your breasts receive extra stimulation. And you and your baby will still enjoy the emotional rewards and benefits of breastfeeding.

Nursing aids can be especially helpful to the employed mother, who may have more than the average share of supply problems. You may not have any such problems, but if you do, try using a nursing aid. Two good choices are the AXIcare Nursing Aid (about $20.00) and the Medela Supplemental Nutrition System (SNS) (about $30.00).

Leaking Milk

Leaking is probably the most common problem nursing mothers face, whether they work or not. However, when you face this problem while you are at work, away from the privacy and convenience of your own home and family, you may feel additional frustration and even embarrassment.

First of all, leaking is really only a minor problem. For most new mothers, the fear of leaking and being embarrassed is greater than the problem itself. While you may feel self-conscious, especially at first, realize that other people don't pay that much attention. And you can handle any difficulty discreetly, without feeling embarrassed, once you understand the problem.

Leaking can occur any time you are very full or have a letdown. It is most common in the early weeks of nursing but may persist longer for some women. It does diminish with time, as your supply becomes more finely tuned to demand.

If you discover that you are leaking, there are a couple of easy things you can do without drawing attention to yourself. If you begin to feel that familiar tingle associated with letdown, you know you may begin to leak. You can stop your breasts from leaking by simply pressing against your nipples; the milk can no longer flow. You can do this without looking obvious by crossing your arms and pressing them against your breasts. If you are sitting down, rest your chin in your hand and press your breast inconspicuously into your arm.

If leaking is a big problem for you, wear nursing pads inside your bra. This is a simple but effective way to avoid leaking through your clothes and causing unnecessary embarrassment.

Most drug stores sell disposable nursing pads, including Medela, Evenflo, Curity, or Johnson & Johnson brands. Disposable pads are the best for preventing sore nipples, because they won't lock moisture in against your skin. Disposable pads cost less than ten cents apiece.

You can also purchase reusable cloth nursing pads, such as those made by

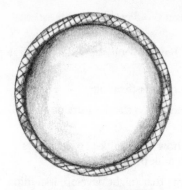

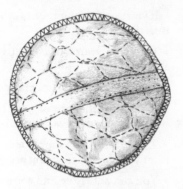

Disposable Nursing Pads

Disposable nursing pads are available in most pharmacies. Avoid plastic-lined pads, which hold in moisture and contribute to sore nipples.

Reusable Nursing Pads

Reusable nursing pads can be washed and reused. You can buy them or make them at home by cutting up diapers into circles and then sewing several layers together.

AXicare. These pads have a 100 percent cotton lining and a moisture-proof polypropylene outer layer that will keep your clothes dry. They cost over a dollar apiece, so you may want to try making reusable clothing pads out of diapers, handkerchiefs, or other similar cotton fabric.

We don't normally recommend using pads with a plastic liner, because they trap moisture and foster sore nipples. But at work, where you don't want to risk obvious leaking, plastic-lined pads are very effective. Just be sure to change them when they become wet.

Whatever type of pad you use, change them as soon as they become wet to avoid irritating your nipples. Also, wet pads won't absorb any more milk.

You might also keep an extra blouse or a sweater or vest at work, just in case you need to change. Keep in mind that a wet spot is less noticeable on a patterned blouse than a solid one; light and clingy fabrics will also show wetness more.

Summary

To really learn how to do something, you must first understand the principles behind it—what it involves and why it works. When learning about breastfeeding, this means understanding how your body works to respond to the needs of your child:

• Your milk supply is "programmed" by your baby's demands.

- If you care for your breasts properly, you can avoid problems with soreness, infection, and supply.

- Care for yourself overall to ensure that you will be able to nurse successfully.

You will also want to understand the basics of breastfeeding:

- Positioning the baby on your breast is essential to effective nursing and will help alleviate soreness, as well.

- The principle of supply and demand—how your milk supply adapts to meet your baby's changing needs—controls milk production.

- You can anticipate and solve any problems that might develop, including engorgement, soreness, infection, lack of supply, and leaking.

Once you have mastered the principles, you can go on to the actual practice. And you can do so knowing that you are prepared and ready. You will be off to a good start!

Chapter 3

Preparations for Mother

After you have your baby, life will never again "get back to normal." The change from employed woman to employed mother is a big one—a permanent one. But you will adjust, adapt, and go forward. And eventually, you will move through this transition and carve out a new "normal" life.

The transition is the tough part. You will grieve for the past's familiar routine and feel anxious about the future's unknown, as you sit uncomfortably between two lifestyles. You can move ahead with certainty, feeling in control, if you do all you can to prepare. We can't overemphasize the practicality of adequate preparation for this stressful adjustment in your life. So use the time before the baby comes to prepare—your work, your home, your wardrobe, and your supplies.

Your Work

Because you are clearly in touch with the demands of your job and want to continue to feel like a valued employee, you will face a good deal of pressure about making arrangements for missing work while you have your baby. On the other hand, this is one area of preparation that may seem a little more concrete because you know what arrangements are necessary. And it is easier to prepare for the "knowns" than the "unknowns."

Maternity Leave

Maternity leave is such a sensitive subject! Devoted career women worry about their long absence from work, while dissatisfied employees complain about not having enough time at home with their baby. Most women are ambivalent about the whole subject. And even going through the experience does not provide all of the answers.

You will get a lot of advice. "Take a long leave." "Take a short leave." "You will be bored." "You won't have a minute of free time."

But the truth is that every woman and every baby and every birth are so different that no one can predict how you will handle all the particular circumstances of your birth and early days or how you will feel about your time at home. Not even you.

Of course, the purpose of leave is to allow you to make a smooth transition into motherhood. Always keep this purpose in mind! For your boss, your friends, your colleagues, and even your partner may not realize this purpose or will at least tend to forget it often. Remind those around you of why you're on leave. You are not on vacation—you are experiencing one of the most significant events in your life and need the time to make a major lifestyle shift. So use your maternity leave to your own advantage.

Many employers are finally beginning to see the advantages of offering family-centered benefit programs, including good maternity plans. For instance, consider these companies:

• Apple Computers, where women hold one-half of all managerial positions, offers job sharing, flexible hours, and six weeks' paid maternity leave.

• Federal Express gives women employees full pay for the first five days of maternity leave and a hefty 70 percent for up to 26 weeks of leave.

• Merck, the nation's largest producer of prescription drugs, offers six weeks' paid leave and up to 18 months of unpaid leave (benefits remain intact) for **both** new mothers and new fathers.

Granted, these are some of the best plans in the country. Your employer may or may not have such a good plan or any plan at all. Regardless of the circumstances, it is up to you to make arrangements for your leave with your employer.

Negotiating your leave should be a high priority, right? Did you even know that maternity leaves could be negotiable? Do you know your legal rights regarding maternity leave? By knowing your rights, planning carefully, and operating tactfully, you will vastly minimize anxiety over negotiating your maternity leave.

In 1978, Congress passed the Pregnancy and Disability Act, an amendment to Title VII of the Civil Rights Act, which states:

Women affected by pregnancy, childbirth, or related medical conditions shall be treated the same for all employment related purposes, including receipt of benefits under fringe benefit programs, as other persons not so affected but similar in their ability or inability to work.

This action changed the legal definition of *pregnancy*, making it a disability. Thus, legally, employers must treat pregnancy the same as they would treat an illness or injury. And this applies to all employment-related practices, including hiring, leaves, promotion, reinstatement, and so on. In addition, employers are barred from instituting a mandatory leave at a specified point in pregnancy when it is not based on the individual's inability to work.

Note that the law does not mandate any specific disability policies, including length of leave and amount of pay received. It only guarantees equality of treatment: Pregnant individuals will be treated the same as other disabled individuals. So your company is still free to form its own policies regarding insurance benefits, paid versus unpaid time off, and the like. But whatever the policies, they must be the same for the pregnant woman as they are for the man with the heart attack.

Earlier, we looked at the leave policies of several large companies. Many small companies simply do not have any policies for disability leave, which is perfectly legal. Actually, this may work to your advantage. If you can conceive and implement a very good plan, everyone wins: You get what you want, a significant precedent has been set for future disabled workers, and the company comes out looking good, too.

Before you begin to negotiate your own leave, check out your company's policies. Find the answers to these questions:

- What are the eligibility requirements (time on the job, management level, etc.)?
- How many weeks' leave am I entitled to?
- Can I add vacation or sick time due?
- What medical reports are required?
- What procedure must be followed to submit a request?
- What are the requirements for filing an extension?
- What arrangements can be made if I want to come back early?
- What are the job guarantees (same job, similar job, same shift, etc.)?
- What constitutes a violation of leave (other employment during leave, etc.)?
- What benefits are provided during paid and/or unpaid leave?
- Are there any other options offered that I am not familiar with?

Once you have all of this information, plant your intentions firmly in your mind and begin to plan your "best-case" leave. Consider all of your priorities: your own needs and interests, the baby's needs, your partner's wishes, your financial situation, and your employer's opinion. And although you can't plan for them, consider the possibility of any unpredicted events. This is a formidable task. Don't take it lightly. Formulate many possibilities; then put the best ones in writing to help clarify your thoughts. Make sure to start planning early so you have enough time to let each plan sit for awhile while you think it over. Try not to solidify your plans too soon, and certainly don't rush in and announce your plan to your boss until you've really taken the time to make the right decision. It's fine for you to change your mind about what you want four times before making a final decision. But you will feel pretty silly (and look highly incompetent) if you go to your boss four times with your latest decision.

Although your and your family's needs are clearly important, try to think from a management point of view as you develop your plan. For the better your plan meets the needs of your employer, the better reception it will have when you present it. An employee who comes in unprepared and whines, "Gee, you owe me this leave," will elicit no cooperation from her employer, even if her work has been good to date. But the employee who comes in and says, "I have a positive plan for seeing that my work continues when I take my leave," will elicit her employer's cooperation, as well as appreciation.

Any employer would like to see a pregnant employee take the following steps in preparation for a maternity leave:

• Develop an attitude of cooperation among your peers by pitching in during others' vacations or sick days to keep up with workloads.

• Stay on top of your own workload during pregnancy. If possible, try to get ahead of things without creating extra stress or making yourself overly tired.

• Discuss your upcoming leave with your colleagues and address any questions or problems they may have. Keep in mind that they are probably not looking forward to the extra work that will be created by your absence.

• Train your fill-in person well. Withholding necessary information out of anxiety about being replaced is self-defeating behavior. Instead, consider that if you train your fill-in well and he or she does a good job during your absence, you will be looked on favorably by your employer and co-workers.

• Make arrangements to stay in touch at work. Call in once a week, accept calls from work after two weeks at home, ask that memos and other important correspondence be sent home to you, and do anything else you are able to do to stay in touch.

Your employer's primary concern about your leave is how your work will get done. In planning for your leave, you should assume the responsibility for getting your work done. If you can come up with a good plan, you will have done the most you can to earn the respect and cooperation of your employer. Your take-charge, problem-solving attitude will be remembered for a long time.

Once you have investigated your company's leave policies, considered your own needs and interests, and prepared your best plan, you are ready to present it to your boss. Don't ever drop in unannounced, even if you work at a small, informal company. Make an appointment and explain the purpose of the meeting to your boss in advance.

When you meet with your boss, listen to the company's position. Consider both the best and worst cases from the "other side." And as you listen, try to read between the lines and sort out your boss' priorities.

Then make your proposal—your best-case plan first. This way, you'll have enough room to negotiate. If your employer agrees to your best case right away, wonderful! If not, you will have a backup plan ready to present immediately. You should go in with a give-and-take attitude, but be confident that you have devised a plan that is truly good for all parties concerned.

In the unlikely (but very uncomfortable) case that your boss seems willing to accept only a plan that seems entirely unworkable for you, stop the meeting. Take a time-out. Excuse yourself, explaining that you'd like some time to think about a plan that you had not previously considered, and make an appointment to meet again. Don't let yourself be pressured into accepting a plan that feels wrong for you. Take enough time to think everything over before you accept or reject a less-than-satisfactory offer.

One professional woman whose employer had no policy or precedent, began formulating her maternity leave plan with clear goals in mind. She wanted to have time with her baby, maintain her promising career, and establish a positive precedent. Since she had to negotiate from scratch, her story can give you an idea of how creative and positive one can be:

I waited as long as possible to tell anyone I was pregnant, in order to preserve my image as a serious professional. Then I made sure that my boss heard the news first, and from me. I carefully planned the first meeting with my boss, and told her the news in a way that again preserved my professional image. And I worked hard to create goodwill among my colleagues.

The plan that I eventually decided on was accepted easily, and became the office policy after that. I based my plan around a three-month leave. For the first three weeks, I phoned in some, but rarely, and had my mail sent to me. At three weeks, I began to accept calls from the office during a specified two-hour period each day. At six weeks, I began accepting calls from clients, as well. From six weeks to three months, I stopped in at the office and brought little bits of work home, but the load was very light. Then, finally, at three months, I began to work part time, at an hourly rate equal to my salary divided by the number of hours in a year.

The plan was wonderfully gradual. My employer was willing to go along with me partly because I had also made some commitments to her. I committed to make some appearances to complete work in progress, even if it occurred in the very early weeks. I committed to working over my regularly scheduled part-time hours when necessary. My work is just not the kind you can drop at noon, saying, "I just work part-time." And I promised to find flexible daycare, so that daycare would never be cause for me to need to leave at a specified point in the day.

With a carefully thought-out plan, and some significant commitments from me, my employer was willing to go along with my very liberal leave plan. For me, the issue was never "How do I get as many weeks with pay as possible?" but rather "How do I arrange my career to match my priorities at this point in my life, without losing steam?" I did it.

The hardest part about a maternity leave is the unknown, the things you can't plan for. Strong, healthy women may have complications and recover slowly, requiring extended leave. And women who couldn't wait to be home with their babies have been known to grow bored and be ready to return to work in three weeks. Still others—dedicated, overachieving, career types— who were initially eager to be back at work after three weeks' leave have ended up continually delaying their return and then finally quitting to stay at home with their babies full time.

No matter how well you plan or how certain you feel about what you want, expect the unexpected. Plan for the outside limit in every instance, just in case. If you ask for a six-week leave but then extend it by 30 days three times, you may just extend yourself into unemployment. But if you ask for a three-month leave and then decide to return earlier than that, your employer cannot help but be flattered and make at least a subconscious note of your dedication.

Once you get that long-awaited leave, make the most of it!

• Heed the advice of everyone—from your doctor to your partner to your relatives and friends—who tells you to do **nothing** but rest, recover, and take care of your baby during your first weeks. This is good advice!

• Take at least all of the leave time your employer offers. If possible, take more.

• Don't give in to the feeling that, since you are not "working," you should take care of all the household duties. Institute or continue shared home responsibilities. (See the section "Your Home" later in this chapter, pp. 41–49.)

• Stay in touch with your work but don't overdo it. Arrange a "phone hour" with your office, a prearranged time at which it is convenient to reach you. And assure people that they really can call you at home.

• When you find the chance for some seemingly decadent relaxation, take it. This is the time to read, watch TV, or take a nap every day. Or spend time just watching your baby sleep.

Adjusting to the Change

Most women can sum up their transition from working person to working mother in one word: **guilt.**

We have found that few women simply drag through their work, feeling dissatisfied and taken advantage of. Quite to the contrary, most women enjoy what they do and feel a sense of commitment and loyalty to their employer.

Any conscientious employee will feel at least a little guilty any time something else gets in the way of her responsibilities at work. "I'm sorry, but my dentist couldn't see me at lunchtime, and I need the afternoon off." "I know that this is a busy period for the company, but I need two days off because my husband is having surgery." Although these are both legitimate reasons for asking for some personal consideration, most devoted employees still end up feeling guilty.

For the employed mother, there is even more of a conflict. Naturally, these women don't want their work performance to suffer once they have a baby. On the other hand, all parents want the best for their child and worry about the effect of their own actions on their child's well-being.

As a working mother, you are committed to two important yet time-consuming roles: employee and parent. You will feel split between the two—all the time. Although this may seem odd, you will probably have many of the same feelings for both your work and your baby. You may feel guilty for not devoting enough time or energy to either one, and you may feel resentment for the demands either one places on you.

Expect to feel guilty. And remember that having mixed feelings, including resentment, doesn't mean that you are not a good mother or a good worker. In fact, it usually means that you **are** both a dedicated, caring employee and a dedicated, caring mother.

Just be wary of acting out of guilt alone, or you will easily be sucked into a defeating cycle. Feeling guilty about not doing quite enough as a parent or a worker may make you try to do more than you can reasonably do. And since there are only 24 hours in a day, if you take on more in one area, you will do less in another. Thus, the cycle: Working causes you to feel guilty about parenting, so you try to do more parenting. But more parenting means less time and energy for working, so you feel guilty about working.

You can avoid this trap by always being honest and realistic about the demands and priorities in your life. And when you do have a guilt attack about working at all, consider the following:

• If you didn't work, your child might not have the basics of life, including enough food to eat or clothing to wear.

• If you didn't work, your child might not have the "extras," such as dance or music lessons or participation in sports.

• If you didn't work, your child might not have you as a role model of self-worth and achievement.

• If you didn't work, your child might feel suffocated and resent your complete preoccupation with his life.

• If you didn't work, you might be bored out of your mind!

When you become an employed parent, you will find some practical adjustment in your daily life, too. You will have more demands placed on your time, and you will have more details to remember about things that may seem new and strange. These tips may help ease this adjustment for you:

• Learn about babies before your baby is born. Read as much as possible. And get some actual experience by babysitting a small baby, if possible. Be sure to involve your partner, too.

• Join groups or take classes that appeal to you, such as La Leche League and childbirth education. Doing so will help you shift to your "parent" mentality. If you can find any "preparing for parenthood" types of classes, by all means, take them.

• Communicate freely and openly with your partner. It is amazing how different a mother's and father's expectations may be. It's also amazing how easily you can leave expectations unexpressed. Share everything—hopes and fears.

• Cut back on social obligations before the baby is born. Both you and your partner will have far less time for your bridge club, bowling league, and Sunday brunch group. But don't eliminate everything. You should both keep one part of your life that's just for you.

• Try to find a support group or a social group that is geared to working parents. You may have to form one yourself. The best source of support is often the circle of friends you will form with other new parents. You can get together and socialize at your various homes—bringing the babies along, of course. Having friends who share your interests in the marvels of babyhood and challenges of parenthood is very important. Of course, this doesn't mean you have to give up your childless friends or quit doing things that don't involve your children. But you'll probably find yourself gravitating toward new parents like yourselves.

• Be flexible and keep an open mind. With anything new, it is easy to have unrealistic, overoptimistic expectations. And it is also easy to feel frustrated or disappointed when your expectations aren't met. Be prepared for your new life as a parent to be different than what you may expect.

• Try to arrange a leave that is a little longer than you think you'll really need—just in case. The standard six-week leave may be a little short. A three-month leave gives you more time to recover physically from giving birth and to pull yourself together emotionally before you face the additional stress that will come with your return to work. Keep in mind that the length of your leave is affected by many factors: your job, your company, your partner, your financial status, and your birth experience. Different mothers will experience different circumstances and need different amounts of time before returning to work.

• When you do return to work, keep the mother side of you in low profile. Doing so will help you reestablish your professional image more quickly. This doesn't mean you need to deny or ignore the fact that you're a mother. But remember, at work, your primary role is that of worker.

Your Home

Although making arrangements for work will probably be your primary concern as your prepare for the baby, don't forget to make arrangements at home, too. Discuss these arrangements with your partner and other family members, as well, and formulate specific plans, as you did with your job.

Streamlining Home Care

You may or may not be a good housekeeper, and you may or may not **want** a clean house. You may share home maintenance with a partner, or you may be a single parent. Whatever your circumstances, count on having less time than ever for home care once your baby is born.

While most of us feel better in a nice, clean house, many of us invest too much time and effort in housekeeping. You can probably lower your standards somewhat and still have a clean, comfortable home. Besides, will having a few more dust bunnies actually change the way you live? Does having a spotless home really make you a better person?

Before the baby is born is the perfect time to streamline your home care routines and clarify your priorities. But before doing so, clear your mind (and your conscience!) of the old-fashioned notions about housekeeping that have been passed on through countless generations of women. If you think you've already cast off these notions, consider the number of chores you do simply because your mother always did them and instructed you to do them, too. A teacher we talked to explained how she grew up washing down the bathroom walls every week when she cleaned the tub, according to her mother's instructions. It took her many years as an adult to realize that this was probably overdoing it by quite a bit. Decide for yourself what housekeeping chores are important and why. Then formulate a plan for accomplishing these chores in an efficient, stress-free manner.

It may help to approach this planning as you would if you were planning something at work. How would you plan for home care if it were your job? Can you find ways to do things more efficiently? Can you see where your priorities are out of line? Are you putting too much time and effort into tasks that are of little or no importance?

It may also help if you try to remember what you thought about housekeeping when you were a child. In most cases, when your mother asked you to do some cleaning, the end result did not look much different than when you began. This made it easy to cheat, right? You could do what she asked very hap-hazardly, and she couldn't even tell the difference. Try your childhood clean-ing methods now, doing everything in the easiest, fastest way possible.

Look for the tasks in your home care routine that are either completely un-necessary or can at least be reduced significantly. And once you've made this evaluation, streamline. Cut-out all the "fat."

What jobs can be done less perfectly?

• Abandon daily bedmaking altogether. Or if that's too drastic for you, prac-tice being a child about it: See how fast you can yank the sheets up, fluff the comforter, and toss the pillow to the top. Believe it or not, you will still have the appearance of an uncluttered bed. And you will save a precious few min-utes over your old hospital corners routine. Besides, who sees your bed while you are at work all day anyway?

• Don't dry the dishes after you wash them. They will air dry quite nicely. Contrary to what you have heard on television, no one has ever died from having waterspots on their glasses!

• Learn to avoid needless steps in doing the laundry. In particular, get away from endless folding and stacking. Just toss socks, underwear, and most baby clothes from the basket into the drawer.

What jobs can be done less often?

• Vacuuming is the best example of a job that can be put off. If you vacuum every day or two, try going a whole week without. If you vacuum every week, try quickly hitting just the high-traffic areas every other week. Don't include seldom used areas in your regular routine; try doing them lightly on occasion. If possible, invest in a small carpet sweeper to use for quick touch-ups, rather than dragging out your vacuum every time.

• Dusting is another overdone chore but one that we have been conditioned to do regularly. Unless someone in the house is allergic to dust, try dusting less frequently and less rigorously. For instance, try dusting just the tops of things every other time you dust. What you can't see won't hurt you.

• Windows. If you are such a compulsive cleaner that you have a regular win-dow-washing routine, you can probably double the amount of time between washings. Perhaps just do windows on a seasonal basis, or do the insides but not the outsides. Or hire them done. Or don't do them at all!

What jobs can you retrain yourself to do more efficiently?

• Replace the standard sheet-changing routine with one that eliminates fold-ing completely. Strip the bed, wash and dry the sheets, and then remake the bed using the same sheets, fresh from the dryer. This way, you won't waste any extra time on folding and putting away sheets.

• To save time sorting laundry, use two hampers: keep one in the bathroom for whites and one in the bedroom for colors.

• Keep a basket at the bottom of the stairs in which you put all of the clutter that needs to go upstairs. Then when you do have to go upstairs, take the basket and put the things away. Save yourself from running up and down the stairs all day.

• Try to implement some of the many timesaving household hints you've heard. You'll be surprised at how easily you can develop new, efficient habits if you make an effort.

• Post a grocery list and add to it immediately when you realize that you're out of something or will need something special. Getting organized at home will save trips to the store for forgotten items. You'll also save money if you stick to your list and avoid unplanned purchases.

• Learn to cook double batches of some dishes, and freeze extra batches for later use. Also plan nutritious meals that involve only one or two courses, rather than those that require preparing several separate dishes.

How else can you save time and energy on housework yet still maintain sufficient order?

• Before you leave for the day, grab a paper bag or a basket and make a fast trip through the house, picking up all the clutter and sticking it in a closet. Then, when you come home at night, the house will be clean and inviting. Empty the bag or basket later or all at once on Saturday.

• Place a basket inside each person's bedroom door, including the baby's. Then, rather than wait for each person to pick up his own things, anyone can pick up anyone else's belongings and simply drop them into the owner's basket. This way, everyone can help keep the house clean. (You and your partner must have separate baskets!)

• Keep a note by the phone, listing any small, nagging tasks that need to be done, like cleaning the top of the refrigerator or polishing candlesticks for an upcoming anniversary dinner. Whenever you talk on the phone, you can work on these little projects. This tactic works for television watching, too.

How can you streamline baby-related tasks?

• Keep "baby-care stations" stocked in several areas of your house. For example, keep diapers, changing equipment, extra baby clothes, and a few toys in baby's room, your bedroom, and the family room. This way, a quick diaper change is always convenient.

• Set aside a spot in your kitchen for milk-pumping supplies, like the pump, bottles or bags, something to label the stored milk with, "blue ice," and your bag or ice chest for transporting the milk.

• After the newborn stage (when babies move their bowels at night), forget about diaper changes during the night. Just pick up your baby, nurse, and go back to sleep. A nighttime disposable or double-cloth diaper will get your baby through the night just fine.

• Make your baby's bed in layers—a waterproof pad, a sheet, a pad, a sheet, a pad, and a sheet. That way, when the sheet needs to be changed—which often happens at night when baby wets—you can hold the baby in one arm and pull up the soiled set of sheet/pad with your free hand. The next layer of sheet and pad is then exposed, already warm, and you can simply lay the baby back down.

• Although baby care will consume a great deal of your time and energy, for your mental health's sake, try to do at least one small thing for yourself each day. Read a chapter in a novel, take a walk, or have cookies and milk all by yourself. Whatever you choose, you will be better able to nurture if you have nurtured yourself a little, too.

Sharing Responsibility

Although the idea of men doing housework is no longer novel, the cold truth is, study after study shows that, in most homes—even those in which both partners are employed—women do most of the home care work. A recent Harris Poll revealed that, in two-career families, women put in 85 hours a week (paid and unpaid work) while men put in 65 hours a week.

Why? Many reasons are offered. Some of these reasons are true, some are merely perceived as being true, and some are blatantly not true. Nonetheless, whether the reason is a social norm or just a problem in your home, it is time for a change.

A few key elements make shared responsibility work well.

1. Both partners must be cooperative. You will not get anywhere with an uncooperative partner.

2. Both partners must be communicative. There are many subtle issues surrounding housework and sharing responsibilities. Careful, tactful communication is necessary to avoid conflict.

3. Both partners should have similar philosophies and priorities. At the very least, their thinking must be compatible.

Having a baby clearly puts stress on your family. And during times of stress, we often revert to the old, comfortable feelings and behaviors that were part of our upbringing. For instance, if your mother always gave you soda and chicken soup when you were sick as a child, you probably still expect it today when you are an adult. Your family may adjust to the stress of having a new baby in a similar fashion. Even though your family may normally share home care, during this time of stress, you may fall back on the gender role stereotypes that were part of your childhood: Mother will run the house and take care of the children, while Father sort of paces the periphery and "helps out" whenever he can.

Even when both partners agree to sharing home care, implementing a workable plan is difficult. But since sharing parental and household responsibilities is so vital to the health of the family as a whole (and certainly to that of its individual members), this challenge deserves serious and direct attention from both partners. You cannot expect your family to live together happily when there are continual conflicts and frustration over sharing responsibilities. Only a joint plan—formulated and agreed upon together and full of compromise and goodwill—provides the structure needed to make home care parity part of your way of life.

You can use a number of methods to devise your plan for sharing responsibilities:

• The "Who Hates Which Jobs Least" method allows the partners to pick the chores that they dislike the least and can do without difficulty. For instance, if you absolutely hate vacuuming, maybe your partner won't mind taking this one. You can volunteer to do his most-hated job. This method increases the odds that the job will actually get done.

• The "I Like These Things Done My Way" method allows everyone to do those chores that they are really picky about. For instance, if you want certain clothes laundered or dried a certain way, do them yourself, rather than gripe that your partner doesn't meet your high standards. This method helps prevent unnecessary tension.

• The "Everyone Rotates" method works around a schedule of various chores that are rotated periodically, so that no one is stuck doing one thing forever. This way, everyone has to take a turn at cleaning the bathroom!

• The "Put Up, Shut Up, or Do It" method prohibits you from asking someone else to do something that you think needs doing. If the dirty dishes in the sink bother you, do them. Don't ask someone else to do them, and don't complain.

Of course, each method has its pros and cons. You may find your own best method by combining certain elements of each.

Even after you've formulated your basic plan, remain flexible. Don't ever write out your routine of duties in ink! You will surely alter it time after time as you continue to adapt and work toward the best solution for your family. Be sure that each partner truly feels in full agreement with the plan, or you may find some subtle sabotage going on in the future.

Also keep in mind that what's best for everyone may change over time. For example, right after the birth of your baby, you will be tired, consumed with baby care, and not able to perform much of the household work. Just recuperating and nursing will probably take most of your energy. During this period, your supportive partner will need to do more than half of the home maintenance work (and that work will have grown in far greater proportion than seems possible with only the addition of one tiny person!). Gradually, as your strength returns and your baby falls into some kind of schedule, you will be able to assume more of your share of the work load.

Although your partner won't be feeding the baby, it is important that he be included in child care from the beginning. All tasks other than feeding can be performed as well by Dad as by Mom, so do share bathing, changing, and comforting the baby from birth on.

Once baby is a little older, many couples actually schedule alternating shifts or days of "Primary Parent" time as part of their plan. Each parent is scheduled times to be "on call" for any baby need. Unless a schedule like this is imposed, many families find that Mommy ends up handling every diaper change, every scraped knee, every neat bug in the grass, every drink, and every spill. This constant responsibility places huge and unfair physical and emotional demands on the mother.

The possibilities for dividing child care and home care duties are really endless.

• While one partner prepares and cleans up after dinner, the other plays "Primary Parent," providing play, bath, and bedtime story. Rotate daily.

• Each parent spends 30 minutes each evening on assigned tasks, while the other parent assumes responsibility for the children. This way, small chores are taken care of during the week, freeing the weekend for the family to spend together.

• Saturday morning is designated as cleaning time, no matter what, which keeps work nights free of hassle.

• Alternate grocery planning and shopping weekly, such that one partner guarantees the other baby-free shopping.

Your family should be able to come up with an equitable arrangement for sharing child and home care tasks. Once you have, you should each bear sole responsibility for your own agreed-upon tasks, including **remembering** to do them. For instance, the person responsible for groceries shouldn't have to be reminded that the milk is almost gone. And the peron who does oil changes should keep track of when they are needed and accomplish them without being reminded. Constant reminders sound too much like nagging, and the ill feelings will erode your good plan. Besides, you won't feel relieved of a task if you still have to remind someone else to do it.

Single Parenting

All of these tips on sharing responsibility obviously won't help the single parent. No one will deny that single parents have a more difficult lot. There is simply too much work associated with a home and a baby (not to mention your employment) for one person to handle. If you can't share the load, you must accept the fact that you can't do it all. Lower your standards and learn to prioritize. Do what is most important and what cannot be put off. For instance, caring for the baby, paying bills, and doing laundry are tasks you probably can't get out of.

If you have a support system of friends or family, this is the time to lean on them. Ask for help when you need it, and learn to accept it.

Hiring Help

One sure way to avoid at least some of the arguments about housework is to hire it done. Certainly, many people feel that they cannot afford this option. But consider all of the possibilities before you decide against hiring help. For example, if you can't afford a regular housekeeper or a weekly maid service, maybe you can hire a teenage neighbor to come in for a couple of hours on Saturday. Also consider hiring help for lawn care, grocery delivery, laundry, and window cleaning, to name just a few.

Actually, hiring household help is becoming more and more popular, as more women feel less compelled to try to be Superwoman. It is unrealistic to think that you can—or should—do it all. And you may be surprised to find out that there are many options available, whatever your personal situation.

Take Dana, a self-employed, single parent of two children, who supports herself on a very small income yet chooses to hire a cleaning person twice a month. As Dana explains:

I know I could clean my house, but the peace of mind that comes from not having to think or feel guilty about it makes it worth every penny. I am better at keeping up with the clutter, too, since I never have to worry about the big tasks. No matter how broke I am, I will never again do without hired cleaning.

Some people may look at Dana and feel that, given her circumstances, she is rather extravagant. But others will look at her and see that she has set her priorities and put them into action.

Your Wardrobe

Regardless of where they work, most women are concerned with their working wardrobe. Clothing is even more of a concern for the new mother, as she moves from regular clothes to maternity clothes to postpregnancy/nursing clothes and back to regular clothes again. In particular, the new mother must deal with two related factors: size change during and after pregnancy and adaptability for pumping and nursing.

If you wear a specific type of clothing for your job (like leotards for dancing), you will be very familiar with your attire and the best ways to suit it to your changing needs. But if you wear a uniform, you may need to ask for a new size every few weeks during your pregnancy. If you pay for your own uniforms, this could get very expensive. Talk to your supervisor and suggest that you make some substitutions, like wearing your own maternity slacks or a loose top or jacket that is similar to the uniform.

If you wear street clothes to work, either casual or professional, you have both the advantage of flexibility and the burden of responsibility. The flexibility advantage is obvious: You can choose what you want to wear, based on your own taste in clothing and your desire for comfort. The burden of responsibility is that you must provide and thus pay for all of your own clothing as you move from size to size.

Expect that you will be heavy for awhile as you lose the extra weight from pregnancy. Depending on how soon you return to work, this may not even be an issue. However, most women find that they don't lose weight as quickly as they had thought they would. So at least consider the possibility that you will be a size or two larger than normal when you return to work. You will probably need at least a few outfits that are loose-fitting enough to accommodate your changing shape.

However, there is a catch to this advice: The clothing styles that are most accommodating to size changes are the least practical styles for pumping or nursing, and vice versa. For instance, a loose dress or jumper, without a fitted waist, will see you through several size changes but must be taken off in order to nurse or pump. Actually, a blouse worn with a skirt or slacks allows the easiest access for pumping or nursing, but neither a skirt nor slacks will work when your waistline keeps changing. A wrap-around skirt would work very well, too, but most women can't and don't want to buy a whole wardrobe of wrap-around skirts just to get them through this short postpregnancy period.

Depending on your wardrobe situation and financial status, you may not buy any new clothes, or you may buy just a few. Regardless, do think ahead about your postpregnancy wardrobe. And if you do buy, do so with this period in mind.

There are a few lines of clothing designed specifically for nursing mothers. Although most women are able to make do with their own wardrobe and don't feel the need or the desire to buy nursing clothing, if you are interested, investigate the following companies:

• Babe Too!, Rojean Loucks, Route 1, Box 195, Assaria, KS 67416

For one dollar, you will get a catalog of patterns and ready-to-wear nursing clothing. The dollar is applied to your first order.

• Duo Designs, 4974 North Fresno Street, Suite 394, Fresno, CA 93726

A brochure is available, illustrating ready-to-wear nursing clothing.

- Easy Feed, Inc., Specialty Nursing Fashions, P.O. Box 35238, Phoenix, AZ 85069

A brochure is available, illustrating ready-to-wear nursing clothing.

- Mary Jane Company, 5510 Cleon Avenue, North Hollywood, CA 91609

This manufacturer carries both prenatal and nursing clothing. This line is also available in department stores and maternity, baby, and specialty shops.

All of these clothing lines follow much the same design principle: They incorporate pleats or folds in the front of the top, concealing zippers or other openings that allow for nursing or pumping without removing the garment. Some women find this design very convenient, but the styles and selection available do not fit all women's needs.

One last wardrobe concern is the problem of leaking. You will most likely leak from time to time while you are breastfeeding, and if you also pump at work, you may leak a little more. We discussed how to ward off excessive leaking and deal with feelings of embarrassment and self-consciousness in Chapter 2. In this discussion of wardrobe adaptability, we offer this advice: simply be prepared. It's a good idea to keep a clean, white or other neutral-colored blouse at work so you'll have a spare should you need to change. If you feel self-conscious about drawing attention to yourself by changing, keep a sweater or vest at work, too (and, of course, a box of nursing pads).

Remember, though, that for most new nursing mothers, the fear of being embarrassed by leaking milk is greater than the problem itself.

Your Supplies

The last step in your preparation is to assemble the supplies you will need. For the employed mother, buying a pump is probably foremost in her mind. (See Chapter 5 on basic types of pumps and Chapter 6 for a thorough survey of the types and specific brands available.)

Unfortunately, choosing a pump is still not easy. The type or brand of pump that one woman swears by may not work at all for her best friend. There is no clear pattern or reason as to why different women have different success with different pumps.

There is no way to tell which pump will work for you until you try. And one try will tell you nothing. You'll need to learn how to pump, which means you'll need a bit of practice with the same pump before you can make any decision on how well it works for you. If you are lucky enough to have a friend or two who has a pump, try to borrow it for a week or so and practice before you make your decision to buy one. If you aren't this lucky, you may end up buying more than one pump until you find the one that's right for you.

In addition to a pump, you'll need bottles and nipples. Start out with just a few when you begin to pump and store milk. Wait to see how your baby reacts to the nipple before you buy too many. Because if the baby has trouble, you'll have to try more than one type. (See Chapter 4, p. 70 for more information on bottles and nipples.)

Keep plenty of nursing pads on hand. The reusable kind may be best for work because of the plastic outer liner. Try disposables, too, to see which kind you prefer. Whatever type you choose, you will need many!

You may also want to pack tissue, paper towels, or premoistened towelettes for cleaning yourself or your pump when you are through. If you'll be pumping away from home, consider what supplies will be available there and what you'll need to bring.

Once you are storing and transporting milk, you'll need a few other supplies, too. Even if you have a refrigerator at work in which to store milk for the day, you should invest in a cooler or large thermos to transport the pumped milk to the day care or your home. Reusable "blue ice" is a worthwhile investment because it is so neat and practical. Better yet, look into a cooler that contains "blue ice" right in the lid.

(See Chapter 5 on pumping, storing, and transporting milk.)

Summary

We can't overemphasize the importance of preparing adequately for the birth of your child. Having a baby will bring enormous change to your life. If you acknowledge this change, address your priorities, and make plans to move ahead, you will make the move from employed woman to employed mother with much more ease and confidence.

The most pressing plans you must make concern your work. In particular, you must make arrangements for your maternity leave, considering the needs of yourself, your baby, your partner, your family, and your employer.

• Familiarize yourself with the legal provisions for maternity leave, as well as any policies your company may have.

• Gather all of your information, assess your priorities, and formulate a number of plans, from best to worst case.

• Present your best case to your employer, giving yourself enough room to negotiate and still come out with a satisfactory plan.

• Expect the unexpected and allow yourself a little extra leave time, just in case.

Your preparation for combining working and mothering must also consider how you will adjust to the change, both emotionally and practically.

• Emotionally, you must acknowledge feelings of guilt and even resentment as you learn to balance your roles as parent and worker.

• Practically, you must be flexible and realistic in order to deal with the changes in your life.

Along practical lines, your preparation should include arrangements to make your life easier.

• Evaluate and streamline your home care routine, eliminating unnecessary tasks and performing others less often but more efficiently.

• Work with your family to set up a plan for sharing household and child care responsibilities.

• Consider hiring help for tasks like housecleaning, lawn care, and laundry.

• Keep your wardrobe as adaptable as possible to meet your changing size needs.

A final note: It's important for you to put a lot of time and thought into preparing for the birth of your child. But don't forget what's been said about "the best-laid plans." You can't anticipate everything; thus, you can't plan for everything. So, above all, be realistic and remain flexible.

Chapter 4

Preparations for Baby

The issue most central to every working mother's peace of mind and every baby's well-being is quality daycare. What may be the best daycare for you and your baby may not be the best for another mother and child. Opinions vary.

It's important to me for Abby to be in her own home, with her own toys and her own crib. It's so important that I'm willing to pay half my salary to someone to come into my home and care for her there.

A daycare home is so much more "real life." I think Max benefits from the interactions and siblinglike relationships he has with the other children there. At his daycare home, he's got a baby, a toddler, another boy his own age, and a "big sister." At home, he's an only child. I think a daycare home is the best solution, at least for Max.

Alex used to go to a daycare home but he was very unhappy. He cried in the morning and he said the daycare mother yelled and made him play in the backyard. Now that he's at a daycare center, everything has changed. He's so much happier. A teacher has more time and patience than a woman caring for her own home and children in addition to your child.

These are just a sampling of the various opinions on daycare options. You will have to decide what is the best solution for you and your child, based on a number of factors:

- your child's age;
- your family situation;
- your work situation;
- how much you have designated to spend on daycare;

- what types of daycare arrangements are available to you; and

- your child care priorities.

In addition, you will have to determine your priorities and what qualities you think are important in daycare, including:

- the qualifications of the people who will care for your child—personal and professional—and

- the conditions of the place in which your child will be cared for—safety factors, educational opportunities, social interaction, loving atmosphere, and the like.

In this chapter, we will review a wide range of daycare topics. First, we will look at the number of available options, from in-home care by a parent, relative, nanny, or babysitter, to out-of-home placement in various types of child care centers. As we examine each option, we will look at both the pros and cons, as reported by actual parents, and provide guidelines for seeking out such care.

Second, we will discuss daycare-related topics: introducing the bottle, packing your baby's bag, when your child is ill, how to provide for emergencies, and how to evaluate the ongoing daycare situation. Finally, we will take you through a trial run, in which you plan for and practice your return to work and your baby's start with daycare.

Daycare Options

Consider these facts about where U.S. children are cared for:

- Over 50 percent of the children under three years of age are cared for in other people's homes.

- 47 percent of all three- to six-year-olds are cared for in other people's homes.

- 15 percent of all three- to six-year-olds are cared for in a daycare center.

- 38 percent of all three- to six-year-olds go to nursery school and then spend the remainder of the day with their parents, are cared for by their mother at her workplace, or are cared for by a paid babysitter in their own home.

Consider this fact, as well: While twenty-six million U.S. children have working parents, there are only about 905,000 spaces for children in licensed care centers. Stated differently, there are almost thirty times more children than licensed places to care for them.

While you may be able to find good care for your child in a licensed center, don't think that it's the only option. Review all of the arrangements that are possible before making your decision.

In-home Options
Care by a Babysitter

Pros:

• You avoid the nuisance of packing and transporting your breast milk safely.

• It is convenient not to have to pack up the baby and her belongings every day and take her to a sitter.

• The baby is more secure staying in her own environment.

• A babysitter in your home may be willing to do light housekeeping.

• A babysitter may be willing to work flexible hours, adjusting to your own schedule changes.

• If your child is sick, she can stay home with the sitter and you can still go to work.

• The child can still play with her neighborhood friends.

Cons:

• You really have no way of knowing what type of care your baby is actually receiving.

• People who babysit rarely have any training in child development.

• It is difficult to find a qualified person who is willing to work for the wages a babysitter receives.

• Hiring an in-home babysitter is an expensive form of child care.

• A babysitter may quit frequently, causing continual adjustment for your child.

• If a babysitter is asked to do housework, she may pay less attention to your child, since the effects of child care are less visible to you than those of cleaning.

If you think the advantages offered by an in-home caregiver are worth the cost, begin a careful search for the right individual. A personal recommendation is best, so start with word-of-mouth inquiries, talking to neighbors, relatives, and co-workers.

If you don't have any success in networking, contact the state employment agency for a listing of babysitters. This service is free to both parties and is certainly worth a try.

You might also look up "Work Wanted" or "Services Available" in the want ads or local bulletins. Sometimes qualified people advertise their services. Or place your own ad, advertising the job and any related information.

If you choose to advertise, prepare your ad carefully. Include as much information as possible about what the job involves and what type of person you are looking for, such as:

- your general home location;
- the hours the job will involve;
- what transportation arrangements are expected;
- what duties you expect to be performed;
- the number of children and their ages;
- how much experience you require;
- what references you require; and
- whether you require a nonsmoker.

You want only those individuals who are qualified and truly interested in the job to contact you, so include whatever you think is important. Use your ad as your first screening tool, and save yourself from doing a great deal of unnecessary screening over the phone.

Once your ad has run and you begin receiving calls, your second phase of screening will begin. Run through your list of requirements and ask specific questions over the phone to verify that the person meets your qualifications. Don't assume that, just because they're responding to your ad, they actually meet your requirements. Also answer any questions they might have, providing additional information where appropriate.

If the phone call goes well and you have good feelings about the person, arrange to meet for an interview. But if you feel at all hesitant or uncertain about the person, don't set up an interview. Chances are, you'll feel even more uncomfortable in person. Only invite people you feel enthusiastic about. If you aren't enthused about anyone, don't interview the best of the undesirables; run another ad and start over.

The interview is your final screening process. Be objective. Don't hire someone because they're nice or because you feel sorry for them. And be selective. Stick to your list of requirements and don't compromise. Also cover the following topics:

- *References*: Many people are too "polite" to require references. This is nonsense! Make it clear that you must have references. And then review and follow up on them carefully. Don't hesitate to ask what you want to know: When did she work for you? How long did she work for you? Why did she leave? What was she expected to do? How well did she perform these duties? How old were your children? How did she relate to them? How did they like her? Was she honest and reliable? Was she clean? Did she have any personal problems, including drug use or alcoholism? Do you honestly have any reservations about recommending her?

- *Discipline*: Ask the candidate how she would react in certain circumstances. Ask her what methods of discipline she has used in the past. Explain **exactly** what you would expect for discipline and note her reaction, spoken and otherwise.

- *Pay*: Sometimes an interviewee will offer to do housework for extra pay. Think twice before giving in to this tempting offer. Consider that, while the caregiver is doing housework, she won't be caring for your child.

- *Breastfeeding*: Let the babysitter know that you are breastfeeding and that you will be leaving stored breast milk for your baby's meals (assuming that you will). Go over the procedures you expect her to follow for handling and preparing the milk. Is she supportive? Does she seem to think it's too much bother? If she seems at all reluctant to go along with the extra effort involved in keeping your baby on a breast-milk diet, you probably shouldn't hire her.

Finally, consider what sort of impression the interviewee makes in person:

- *Communication*: Does she communicate well? Does she understand everything you say? Can you understand everything she says? Will she be able to remember and follow directions, including written instructions? If possible, subtly find out how well the applicant reads.

- *Appearance*: How does she look? Is she neat and clean? Does she appear to be healthy? If not, ask about her health.

- *Child Care*: Let the interviewee handle your baby. Does she seem comfortable? Does she seem competent and experienced? Does she seem gentle and caring? How does your baby respond to her? This is one of your best means of judging an applicant, so pay careful attention.

When you find an applicant who seems perfect for the job, hire her and set up an outlined probation period. Then watch closely. If either of you aren't happy with the situation, it's better to start over again than let things deteriorate.

Care by a Relative

Pros:

- The child is cared for by someone who knows and loves her.

- The caregiver is a constant person in the child's life.

- A homelike atmosphere is maintained.

- Care is usually inexpensive and may even be free.

- The child is familiar with the environment.

Cons:

- You may have less input on the care provided, depending on your relationship with the caregiver.

• If your relative is not supportive of breastfeeeing, it may be especially hard to get her to cooperate in handling and feeding the expressed breast milk you leave for your baby.

• If the child is unhappy with the situation, it will be difficult to change day-care arrangements.

• Even small conflicts may cause bad feelings within the family.

• An elderly relative may have physical or energy limitations that restrict what they can offer the child.

Child care provided by your mother, mother-in-law, sister, or other nearby relative is not uncommon. But only you can assess if it's going to be a good arrangement. The bottom line is, will you be able to stay in control of the type of care your child receives? Or, as often happens, will you be unable to impose your ideas on a relative because of your own personal ties?

Before you make a decision on asking a relative to care for your child, consider all of the implications—for you, your child, and the relative.

Care by a Certified Nanny

Pros:

• Certified nannies have good training in child care.

• The child will be cared for in her own home.

• A nanny will become part of your family.

• Nannies are devoted to child care as a vocation.

• A nanny will provide flexible hours and will even be available should you go out of town.

• A nanny may become a long-term employee, offering stability to the child.

• Some nannies do other work, too, like shopping, laundry, and taking children to lessons, doctor appointments, and the like.

• A nanny will most likely have been educated about the merits of breast-feeding and should support your perseverance.

Cons:

• A trained, certified nanny is the most expensive child care option.

• Since nannies are usually live-in help, you will have to provide living space for her.

• You will lose some privacy having a live-in employee.

The nanny is a recent addition to American daycare options. Although she may seem like a live-in babysitter, there is an important difference: A nanny has gone to school and studied child development and other facets of child care. She is also certified.

One nanny school with an excellent national reputation is NANI, the National Academy of Nannies, Inc., in Denver. Young women from all over the country go to NANI to study infant care and stimulation, child psychology, safety and emergency instruction, child development, nutrition, and family relations. The school screens the students thoroughly through psychological testing, tracking academic performance, and evaluating performance in various in-home internships.

A well-trained nanny can assume as much responsibility for the care of your children as you want to give her, from buying appropriate clothes, to choosing safe toys, to giving medication, to providing developmentally appropriate activities, to giving emergency medical attention. She can fill the role of substitute parent.

Hiring a nanny is not a realistic daycare option for many people because of the cost. While you will be hiring someone with good qualifications, you will also be paying her good wages and providing her with room and board.

How do you go about hiring a nanny? The best idea may be to contact a nanny school and let it serve as your placement agency. You will probably be required to pay a placement fee, but you will have the opportunity to interview several candidates and examine their credentials and recommendations. Should you decide to hire one of these individuals, you will probably sign an employment contract with her, which is to your mutual benefit.

If you don't go through a nanny school, you may be able to locate a nanny by running a classified ad. If you are going to pay "nanny wages," ask for proof of the applicant's certification. Again, be sure to get references and check them thoroughly. For an additional reference, you might also contact the school where the applicant trained.

Care by Parents over Staggered Hours

Pros:

• The child is cared for by those who love her the most.

• The child stays in her own home.

• The child can have her friends over to play.

• The parents remain in control of child care.

• Your partner will surely be supportive, helpful, and knowledgeable about feeding the baby breast milk in your absence.

Cons:

- Parents may see less of each other.

- Developing complementary work schedules will be difficult and stressful.

- This is not an option for single parents.

Some parents feel so strongly about always caring for their own child that they arrange their work hours to be complementary, rather than coinciding. Specifically, the parents arrange their work schedules so that one of them will always be able to take care of the child. For instance, the mother may work days and the father may work evenings.

Quite clearly, depending on the type of work the parents do and the number of hours they must put in, coordinating schedules like this may be difficult, if not impossible. And since the demands of new parenthood already cut down on a couple's time together, reducing it even more by alternating work schedules to facilitate child care may be especially stressful.

But a great deal of credit must be given to those parents who make this arrangement work. They are certain that their child is receiving the best possible care, and they are saving a good deal of money, too.

This is probably the best child care situation for an infant or toddler. Consider Charlene and Dave, who worked out an alternating arrangement for their toddler son, Eric. Dave goes to work at 8 a.m. and comes home at 5 p.m. Charlene is a nurse who works the evening shift. She goes to work at 2:30 p.m. and leaves Eric in the care of a neighbor for 2½ hours until Dave comes home and picks him up at 5:00 p.m. This cuts down on child care time for Eric and saves Dave and Charlene on child care costs. And since Charlene only works until 11:00 p.m., she and Dave are still able to sleep the same hours. This arrangement has proven to be ideal for this family.

Away-from-Home Options
A Daycare Center

Pros:

- A center remains open, regardless of a single teacher's illness or resignation.

- Peer pressure may cause teachers to perform their jobs well.

- An educational program may be provided.

- There are other children to play with.

- The cost is usually less than that of hiring a sitter.

- Teachers are usually trained in child development.

- A center must adhere to some state safety and health regulations.

Cons:

- Centers often do not accept infants under one year old.

- The center may not be open early enough in the morning or late enough in the evening to correspond with your work schedule.

- Some children need more one-on-one attention than a center provides.

- The turnover of personnel may cause some instability for the children.

- Centers and teachers will vary in their willingness to go along with the storage and preparation of breast milk feedings.

- Illnesses are spread among the children in the center.

- A center will usually not care for sick children.

- A center does not usually offer afterschool care for older children.

We recommend that you visit several daycare centers before making up your mind. Make careful observations during your visit.

- Is the environment—indoors and out—clean, stimulating, and safe?

- What types of activities are provided?

- Do you like the kinds of toys and activities that are provided?

- What type of food is served?

- How do the teachers deal with the children? Are they patient or irritable?

- How flexible are the teachers about individual differences, including temperament, maturity level, personal habits, skills, and needs?

- How do the teachers greet and say good-bye to the children?

- Do you hear the happy chattering of children at play? Or do you hear crying and unhappy sounds or rowdy and unruly play?

- How receptive are the teachers to your bringing in stored breast milk for your baby? Are they experienced in storing and handling expressed milk? If not, are they willing to learn?

Don't hesitate to ask questions during your visit. In particular, ask the director about:

- the hours the center is open;

- any policies regarding late pick-up;

- the teacher turnover rate;

- the training of the staff;

- the teacher/child ratio;

- what insurance coverage the center carries for accidents or injuries;
- the center's own goals for the children;
- what is done to help a new child adjust;
- the discipline policies followed;
- the kinds of activities and outings planned;
- parent visitation policies; and
- the policies regarding sick children.

Finally, discuss any special needs your child has—physical, emotional, developmental, or otherwise. And make it clear that you would expect to receive feedback about how your child is adjusting.

It's a good idea to visit the center more than once. If possible, go at different times of the day. For instance, stop in during lunchtime to see if the meals are really as nutritious as you've been told they are. And observe the general mealtime atmosphere. Is it pleasant or tense?

Another good idea is to take your child with you when you visit the center. Her reaction to this new environment may be especially revealing. And although you must make the final decision, give her impression some weight.

Once you've reviewed all of your observations about the different centers you've visited, use your best judgment and your own gut-level feelings to make a decision. Then, give your child one month to adjust. If things aren't going well, you may want to change centers. Be as involved as you can with the daycare center. Your input can improve the program and allow you to stay in touch with what really goes on.

A Daycare Home

Pros:

- It provides a homelike environment for the child.
- A daycare mother will do better financially operating a home and caring for several children than she will babysitting just one child, so she may be less likely to quit.
- There are other children to play with.
- A home may be the most affordable option.
- A home will accept infants through school-age children.
- A daycare mother may offer flexible hours to meet your schedule.
- A home may be close to either your own home or work.

Cons:

• Daycare mothers are usually not trained.

• The mother will need to spend some time maintaining her house and caring for her own children.

• Unlicensed homes are sometimes overcrowded.

• If the caregiver is sick, you will have to make other arrangements for your child's care.

• Illnesses are spread among the children.

• If no activities are planned, the children may end up watching a lot of TV.

A daycare home is the choice that parents of infants most frequently make, since many daycare centers won't take children less than one year old. Also, many parents feel that their infant will receive more attentive care from a daycare mother than she might in another type of daycare situation.

When you set out to choose a daycare home, try to get personal recommendations. Also visit several homes more than once to observe their operation.

In addition, find out if the home is licensed. Licensing requirements vary from state to state, but generally, they refer to safety inspection issues and the number of infants and children allowed in the home. If you choose a licensed home, you can be assured that your child won't face overcrowded conditions. Beware, though—licensing doesn't tell you anything about the daycare mother's personality or her ability to care for children.

When you visit the prospective home to interview the daycare mother, pay attention to all aspects of the situation.

• *The Home:* Is it large enough for the number of children that are cared for? Are there several areas for the children to use, so they can separate if necessary? Is the house relatively clean? Are there toys and equipment appropriate for your child's age? Is the backyard set up as a play area for the children? Are there pets in the home? If so, what type?

• *Safety:* Are harmful substances such as cleansers, medicines, paints, and gasoline kept locked away and out of children's reach? Are electrical outlets covered and other general safety measures followed? Are the toys provided safe? Are they safe for a baby the age of your child? Is the backyard fenced in? Does the gate have a lock on it? Does the home have insurance that would cover an accident or injury? Are emergency numbers posted? Is there a strict policy to release children to no one other than the parents or another preauthorized person?

• *The Daycare Mother:* Is she friendly? Does she seem like a happy person? Does she seem to like children? Does she pay attention to the information you offer about your child? How many of her own children are at home? What are their ages? How does she treat the other children? Does she give each child individual attention and affection? Is she flexible, patient, and easygoing? Does she seem to have good judgment? Does she seem to resent specific considerations for individual children? Does she talk negatively about other parents or children? Does she provide supervised, structured activities for children? Or are they left mainly to play on their own? How much TV does she let them watch? Are her values and ideas about discipline in line with yours? Does she have any training in child development?

• *Breastfeeding:* Did the daycare mother breastfeed her own children? (If so, she will probably be supportive of your efforts to continue breastfeeding and will be happy to help you.) If the mother didn't breastfeed herself, is she willing to learn how to handle the breast milk you bring? Does the mother seem supportive, or does she think that your efforts are unimportant or unnecessary? Does she object to the extra effort involved in feeding your baby breast milk? Don't hire her if she won't support what's important to you.

• *Policies:* How much does the home charge? How much for overtime? Do you pay when you're on vacation or when your child is sick? What do you do when the mother's sick? How is her health? How flexible is she about late pick-up? What is the policy on sick children?

No home will score perfect points in all of these areas. But how does it rate on most of them?

Ask the daycare mother for the names and phone numbers of some of the parents she works for now. Talking to them will be very helpful to you. If the mother doesn't want to give you the numbers, it may indicate some problem. Ask her to give your name and number to the other parents instead. If she still resists, be suspicious that there is some problem. Whatever the case, don't make a commitment until you've talked to several other parents of children in the home.

If possible, bring your baby along to the home, and observe how the mother interacts with your child. Take their mutual reactions into consideration, too.

Don't make a decision while visiting the home and talking with the mother. Take all your information and impressions home and ponder them for awhile. Again, rely on your instincts. If you feel at all uncomfortable about the mother, her home, her policies, or reports you received from parents—whether you can pinpoint the specific problem or not—heed your intuition. This decision is crucial. Make it carefully.

An Infant Care Center

Pros:

• No baby is too young; infants are accepted from birth on.

• Only infants are cared for.

• The personnel are specifically trained in infant care.

• Some centers offer drop-in services, allowing parents to use the center for sporadic daycare needs, either instead of or in addition to their regularly scheduled daycare.

• Most centers are concerned about offering infant stimulation.

• Some have facilities for sick infants, perhaps even with a pediatric nurse's care.

• The cost is reasonable.

• An infant care center is likely to be experienced in handling expressed breast milk, since they are designed specifically for the care of infants.

• A center will probably be receptive to your dropping in daily to nurse your baby, should you want to.

Cons:

• Illnesses may be passed among the infants.

• Depending on the infant/caregiver ratio, your baby may not receive prompt and adequate attention.

• Since this type of center is new and uncommon, it may be difficult to find one that is conveniently located.

The infant care center is a new daycare option appearing in many cities. This type of center developed in response to a previous void in the child care market: Many families have infant children, and few daycare centers accept infants.

These centers accept only infants, usually from birth to eighteen months. Their rates are similar to those of regular daycare centers, but you enjoy the specialization of infant care.

Cradle Care, in Aurora, Colorado, is typical of an infant care center. It is bright, cheerful, and clean. The director explained that her staff is trained in infant care and development. Each day, a developmental lesson is planned for each baby. The center also has a strict policy that a crying baby is to be picked up immediately and that no baby will ever cry for more than five minutes. This may not be the policy of all infant care centers, so ask about the response to crying infants when you visit a potential care site for your baby.

Cradle Care encourages breastfeeding mothers to come any time and nurse their infants. Some staff members are nurses and can even help with breast-feeding. In addition, the center provides a room for sick infants and a pediatric nurse is on hand for medical attention. Again, this may not be typical, so be sure to ask about the policies of the center you visit.

As with the daycare and home care centers, visit as many infant care centers as possible and carefully observe operation. Ask or look for answers to these questions:

• Are there separate areas for sleeping infants so they won't be disturbed by the noisy ones?

• Does each baby sleep according to her own schedule? Or are all of the babies put to bed at the same time?

• Does each baby have her own crib?

• Are the babies always held when given their bottle? Do you see any propped bottles?

• If you bring in pumped breast milk, will the personnel follow adequate safety guidelines in storing and feeding your baby?

• Is all the baby equipment safe and in good condition? For instance, do all of the infant seats and strollers have safety harnesses?

• Is a safe, clean place provided for crawling babies to play and explore?

• Are the babies changed frequently?

Try to visit a prospective center several times, at different times of the day. Also talk to parents of other infants at the center. If you feel that the infant care center staff is warm and responsive to the babies it cares for, this could be a good daycare option.

The major drawback of infant care centers is that there are not many around. And even if you find one, it may not be conveniently located.

A Daycare Center at Work

Pros:

• You won't make any extra trips to and from work, and you and your baby can enjoy that extra time together in the car.

• You will have greater peace of mind, knowing that your baby is nearby and that you can be easily contacted in case of a problem.

• You will probably be able to nurse your baby whenever you want to, eliminating the need for expressing breast milk.

• Many of the other daycare parents and their children will be familiar to you, since you are co-workers.

• You may be more aware of the functioning of the daycare center and the performance of the personnel, since you are on the same premises. You may also have more input about the center's policies and any changes you think should be made.

• Some employer-run centers are subsidized by the company, making the care they provide more affordable for employees.

Cons:

• You face the same risks regarding the quality of care provided that you face with any daycare arrangement.

• Depending on where and how much your partner works, the location may not always be convenient for you as a couple. As a result, one parent may end up being solely responsible for the daycare arrangements.

Unfortunately, only a few progressive employers provide daycare on the work premises. But those who do realize the benefits it offers:

• Having a daycare center is an asset that will attract employees.

• Providing daycare at work creates goodwill and appreciation among the employees.

• When daycare is provided, the employee turnover rate is lower, because parents are unlikely to pull their child out of a good daycare situation even if they might otherwise be inclined to look for a new job.

• Providing daycare also produces a lower employee absenteeism rate, since parents won't have to miss work when their babysitter or daycare mother is sick or quits.

One important advantage of on-premise daycare for the employed, nursing mother is that it greatly facilitates nursing. Rather than use her breaks and lunchtime to pump, a mother can go to her baby and nurse, instead. This is not only more convenient and pleasurable; it is also faster. Since babies are so efficient at getting the milk out, it actually takes less time to nurse than to pump.

Daycare centers at work should become a growing trend, as parents realize that it is beneficial to have their children near them and are less afraid to assert themselves and request this service of their employer. But establishing a center is not always feasible for an employer. Obviously, it takes a large work force to justify providing daycare.

A book by the Learning Institute of North Carolina, called *Who Cares for the Children? A Survey of Child Care Services in North Carolina*, reports on this subject:

Some companies and unions have set up child-care centers for their own workers. Generally parents pay for this service on a sliding scale, and the company covers the rest. The Skyland Textile Company in Morgantown, North Carolina; KLH, which manufacturers stereophonograph systems and other high fidelity equipment in Cambridge, Massachusetts; and the Amalgamated Clothing Workers in Chicago have all set up centers for their workers' children—and sometimes for the children of other people in the community. It has been found that the establishment of such facilities cuts down on absenteeism and generally improves the morale of women workers who are confident that their children are being well cared for.

Nearly one hundred hospitals have set up child-care centers (some running for twenty-four hours) for the children of nurses and other employees. Some universities provide facilities for the children of their students and faculty—and women's groups are pressing more universities to do the same.

There is another option for those businesses that don't have enough employees to establish their own daycare center: A number of small businesses in the same office building or neighborhood might pool resources and form a sort of cooperative center.

If you work in an establishment that doesn't presently have a daycare center, consider organizing one yourself. Are there enough children to make it worthwhile? Is there enough interest among your co-workers? Would it be possible to combine with other offices in the area? Explore the possibilities and see how far you can go toward creating the best daycare situation for you and your children.

Finding Available Daycare

As we've mentioned throughout, the best way of finding daycare is through a personal recommendation. Ask your friends, neighbors, relatives, and co-workers for help in locating a number of potential daycare situations.

If your networking doesn't come through or you're new to an area, try any of the following organizations for help:

- the United Fund;
- the Community Chest;
- the YMCA/YWCA;
- the National Council of Jewish Women;
- the National Council of Negro Women; and
- the League of Women Voters.

Also try local agencies that sponsor human and family services, including church groups, hospitals, and women's organizations. The Yellow Pages is also a handy reference; look up "Day Care" or "Child Care" for available listings.

Related Daycare Concerns
Introducing the Bottle

Another concern for the new mother who is returning to work is getting her baby to accept the bottle. A working mother cannot have a more disturbing thought than that of her baby shrieking with hunger and unwilling to take a bottle at the babysitter's.

When to Start. The best age at which to introduce the bottle depends a great deal on how much time you have before returning to work. In general, you probably won't want to introduce the bottle before the baby is six weeks old. Six weeks is about the time it takes for a mother's milk supply to become stabilized, so if it all possible, wait at least until then. If you must return to work sooner than six weeks after the baby is born, wait until just before you go back to work to introduce the bottle.

The following schedule provides rough guidelines for when to introduce the bottle, depending on the length of your leave from work:

If you return to work at:	Introduce the bottle at:
6 weeks	4 weeks
3 months	2 months
6 months	3 months

How to Start. How often should you give the bottle? If you will return to work within a few weeks, give the baby one bottle every few days. If you have more time at home, try one bottle a week.

Your baby will probably take less milk from the bottle than she would have from the breast. Offer about four ounces, which is more than your baby is likely to take, so you can see the maximum amount of milk she is willing to take by bottle. She will take more as she becomes more skilled at bottlefeeding.

It is important for your milk supply not to overdo using the bottle. Certainly, you want your baby to accept the bottle, but you also want to build your milk supply. For this reason, when you introduce the bottle to the baby, we recommend that you anticipate a time when she would normally be nursing. Pump your breasts just before you expect the baby to be hungry. Then put that milk into a bottle and use it immediately. If the baby is fed before she becomes extremely hungry, she may be more cooperative about trying something new.

Someone other than the mother should give the baby the bottle. The baby is more likely to accept it from someone else, because she associates her mother with the pleasant sensations connected with nursing at the breast. Because of this, the baby may fight getting milk any other way from Mom.

Actually, this is an advantage and should be reinforced. Since one of the risks of nursing and working is that the baby may reject the breast for the bottle, the exclusive association of the mother with the breast is very helpful. Your partner or caregiver are the most logical people to give the bottle. However, if that isn't possible, choose someone else who feels confident and patient with the baby.

Choosing Bottles and Nipples. The disposable bags used in some feeding systems are not a good idea when using breast milk. An immunological component of breast milk, secretory IgA, is bound and thus rendered unavailable as a result of storage in these bags. Hard plastic or glass bottles are both good choices.

Any type of bottle system is fine for formula. Whatever type you choose, make sure you have enough bottles. The four-ounce bottle is a good size, since you will want to freeze milk in small quantities. While your baby is young, keep about six four-ounce bottles on hand. As she grows older, buy six eight-ounce bottles.

Next, you need to select a nipple.

1. Orthodontic nipples are supposed to be shaped like the breast when it is compressed in the baby's mouth. Although they are touted for their dental benefit, the advantage is probably not significant, especially since your baby won't be bottlefeeding full-time anyway.

2. Playtex Nurser nipples are designed to resemble a human breast and nipple. Many mothers who use the Playtex nipple find that it doesn't have any advantage over other nipples in terms of being more acceptable to a breastfeeding infant.

3. Standard nipples certainly do not look like a human breast or nipple, but most babies seem to like them perfectly well.

Many employed mothers find that the baby can switch back and forth from bottle to breast with less confusion if an orthodontic nipple is used. On the other hand, if your baby doesn't seem to like it, you may have better luck with another nipple. The standard nipple is often accepted just fine.

The Formula Option. Many women are emotionally committed to providing breast milk to meet all of their baby's nutritional needs, even while they're working. Some women work full-time and do successfully pump enough milk for all the baby's feedings.

But other women find that they can't pump enough to supply 100 percent of their baby's milk and must use formula as a supplement while they're at work. And still others choose not to pump at all, preferring to leave formula for their babies.

Should you decide on formula as a supplement, don't feel disheartened. Keep in mind that the major benefit of your continued nursing is the emotionally fulfilling experience that you and your baby enjoy. If you set this as your purpose, rather than worry about letting any formula pass your baby's lips, you will find the whole experience more pleasant and less anxiety producing. And even if you primarily leave breast milk, if you leave some formula at the babysitter's as an emergency backup, you will probably find yourself less pressured and less worried about your baby's hunger.

Discuss choosing a formula with your health care professional. Also consider that medical science has had much more experience with cow's milk formula than with soy formula. So start with a milk-based formula and consider a soy-based one only if problems develop. Almost as many babies are allergic to soy as to cow's milk, so soy is not a great deterrent to allergies.

Many breastfeeding mothers are completely unfamiliar with formula. There are three basic kinds:

1. *Ready-to-feed formula:* This type is ready to use, requiring no dilution or preparation. If you anticipate only occasional use, ready-to-feed formula is a good option. Ready-to-feed formula costs approximately 20 cents per four-ounce serving.

2. *Concentrated formula:* This type comes in a liquid and must be diluted with water at a 1:1 ratio before it is fed to the baby. Once the can has been opened, it must be stored in the refrigerator and is good for only forty-eight hours. Concentrated formula costs approximately 15 cents per prepared four-ounce serving.

3. *Powdered formula:* The powdered typed comes in a can with a scoop. One scoop of formula is mixed with two ounces of water. Powdered formula is the least expensive type and will store easily. It is a good choice for an employed mother. Powdered formula costs just over 10 cents per prepared four-ounce serving.

All formulas come with and without iron. Full-term, healthy babies, especially those who are breastfed, don't normally need extra iron. You should consult your physician about your baby's needs before you decide on a formula.

If you choose to use formula either occasionally or regularly while you're at work, just leave a supply at the caregiver's house. Don't try to guess every morning if and how much formula supplement your baby will need that day. Buy the formula, leave it with the sitter, and let her use it as she needs it.

Once you've chosen a formula, give your baby time to get used to it **before** you go back to work. Try it a couple of times to make sure she doesn't have a bad reaction to it. Since you know what's normal for your child, you are the best person to assess whether her behavior constitutes a bad reaction.

Common Problems. On occasion, a baby may refuse to take the bottle. We offer several strategies for determining what's wrong and what you can do to correct the problem:

• Perhaps you're pushing the nipple into the baby's mouth too aggressively. Try laying the nipple next to the baby's mouth and letting her grasp it herself.

• Your baby may not like the type of nipple you are using. (Some babies are amazingly particular!) Try different types until you find one that she likes.

• Remember, a breastfed baby is used to a body-temperature nipple, and the bottle nipple may be cold. Try running warm water over the bottle nipple before giving the bottle to the baby.

• The hole in the nipple may be too large or too small, giving the baby more or less milk than she wants. Test the nipple by holding the bottle upside down. If the milk pours out, the baby is getting too much. If only a drop appears, even after you squeeze the nipple vigorously, the baby is getting too little. Both situations can be very frustrating for the baby. If the hole is too big, change nipples; if it is too small, you can use a red-hot pin to make the hole bigger.

• If all else fails and your baby absolutely refuses the bottle, have the caregiver feed her using a spoon or eyedropper. Do keep trying the bottle, though. The baby will probably give in soon.

• If your baby is already on solids and reluctant about the bottle, have your sitter put as much liquid as possible into the solid food. For instance, prepare cereal with lots of formula or breast milk.

Packing Your Baby's Bag

If your baby is cared for outside your home, you will need to pack a bag to send with her each morning. Items you should pack in the bag each day include:

• diapers;

• a change of clothing;

• a freshly cleaned pacifier or two (if you use them);

• any special toys;

• medicine, if needed;

• a bib; and

• pumped breast milk (unless you dropped it off yesterday) or formula (if you use it during the day).

Items you may want to leave in your baby's bag permanently include:

• a favorite blanket;

• ointment;

• baby wipe-ups;

• a photo of you and your partner; and

• a spare hat and mittens.

It will be convenient for you to keep large items (like a playpen, swing, or walker) at the babysitter's house. And if you use a daycare center, equipment will be provided. You and your caregiver should make your own arrangements for providing formula, food, and the like.

If you want to monitor the number of diaper changes your baby receives each day, put in a certain number of diapers each day and then count how many are left at night. If you're not worried about diaper changes, it's easier to leave a supply of diapers at the babysitter's and replace it when needed.

When Your Baby is Ill

Your particular caregiver may or may not have policies regarding sick children. Regardless, the real decision is yours: What should you do when your child is sick?

Of course, there will occasionally be badly timed illnesses when it is just impossible for you to miss work. And there will be minor illnesses that won't require you to stay home. But for those times when your baby is really sick, consider that she will be much more comfortable with you, at home, than she would be with a babysitter or at a daycare center. Also consider the message that your staying home sends to your baby: She is more important to you than your work is.

To assess whether your child is sick enough to warrant your staying home from work, ask these questions:

- Does she have a fever?
- Does she have diarrhea?
- Is she vomiting?
- Does she have any severe pain, such as a stomachache, headache, or earache?
- Does she seem weak and lethargic?
- Do her symptoms lead you to suspect that she has something contagious, like impetigo, pink eye, strep throat, or chicken pox?

A positive answer to any of these questions should tell you that you or your partner should stay home with the child. Perhaps a call or visit to the doctor is also in order. Observe your child carefully and pay attention to other differences you notice in her behavior or appearance, since you know her better than anyone else.

Emergency Situations

Every parent dreads the moment of being called at work and told that her child has become ill or been injured. Should you receive such a call, leave work, if at all possible. But should you not be able to leave or get to your child immediately, your child's caregiver must be trusted to handle the situation.

In order for someone other than you or your partner to secure medical care for your child, they must have your permission. You can grant this permission by signing a medical release form, as shown below. It specifies the following:

- the name of the individual to whom you give permission;
- the name of your child;
- the time period in which your authorization is effective; and
- your permission, as indicated by your signature.

Medical Release Form

I hereby grant permission for _____

to authorize medical treatment, both emergency and non-

emergency, for my child, _____, in

my absence. This authorization is effective from _____

to _____.

_____

If your child goes to a licensed daycare home or daycare center, you probably signed such a release when you registered. If you hire someone to care for your child in your home, you should leave them a signed medical release form. If a relative cares for your child, a release form may not be necessary. But just to be on the safe side, it wouldn't hurt to provide a medical release form for anyone who regularly cares for your child.

Be assured, however, that if your child were brought to a hospital emergency room with a true medical emergency, the hospital personnel would treat your child immediately, without waiting for the consent form.

When Things Aren't Going Well

Unless your child can talk, it is difficult to know whether she is happy in her daycare setting. To determine how things are going, look for clues:

• When you drop off your baby in the morning, does she seem happy to see the babysitter? Or does she cry and refuse to go to her?

- When you pick up your baby at night, is she happy and content? Or is she cranky and unhappy?

- Does your baby look clean and well cared for when you pick her up?

- Does the babysitter appear to change the baby's diaper often enough? Does she have diaper rash?

- Has your child become withdrawn? Has she become temperamental, perhaps throwing tantrums?

- Does your child seem to have nightmares?

- How is your child's appetite?

- How is your child's health? Does she get sick more often?

Never fail to ask about an injury to your baby, no matter how minor it may seem. Question the babysitter until you are satisfied that she did not hurt your baby or is not allowing another child to do so, either. Be particularly inquisitive if the story sounds even a little unlikely.

Keep in mind that no daycare situation is absolutely perfect, and no child is happy and pleasant all of the time. And keep in mind that crankiness, health, and appetite can also be affected by things that have nothing to do with the daycare—like teething.

You may also have to balance your priorities. Perhaps your babysitter is wonderful and warm and rocks your baby to sleep but doesn't wash her face after lunch. What is more important to you? Just don't compromise anything that will affect your child's safety or well-being.

If, after reviewing the situation carefully, you feel that your baby is being poorly cared for or even being hurt or neglected, withdraw from the arrangement immediately. Too many good, concerned parents have brushed off potential warning signs of problems because they just couldn't believe anything was really wrong. Yes, it is difficult to start all over again and search for quality daycare. But that is your responsibility as a parent. The guilt of not doing so will be far greater than the effort of the search.

The Final Countdown

It's about a week before you will return to work. You've hired a babysitter, made all the necessary arrangements at work, and stored some breast milk in the freezer. Now comes your "trial run."

Your first day back to work and your baby's first day with her new caregiver will both be difficult. So don't attempt both "firsts" on the same day. In particular, give your baby a chance to get a little familiar with her new surroundings before she begins her first whole day.

About a week before you return to work, make arrangements to leave your baby with her new sitter for a short amount of time. For this first visit, choose a time that does not include a feeding. A few days later, arrange to leave the baby for a couple of hours, including a feeding time. This will give the babysitter a chance to thaw and give a bottle of breast milk while carefully following your detailed instructions. You should be available for a phone call to answer questions or discuss problems.

Also use these introductory days to prepare yourself. Keep in mind that your morning routine will now include a few more steps than it did before. To help you plan how much time you'll need in the morning, see how long it takes you to:

- get yourself ready;
- eat breakfast;
- nurse the baby;
- get the baby dressed and ready to go;
- pack the baby's bag;
- nurse the baby again at the sitter's; and
- settle the baby in at the sitter's.

Add up the minutes for each of these activities, and then add in how long it takes you to get to work. Then add at least an extra fifteen minutes for last-minute emergencies, like a diaper or outfit change.   Now figure out what time you'll need to get up in the morning.

Make a trial run at least once. If possible, run a few trials in order to develop the most efficient, complete routine possible. Doing so will make life easier for your baby, as she will not suddenly be immersed in a new and strange environment. And it will also make life easier for you, as you'll feel less stressed and better able to handle your first days back at work.

Summary

Our look at daycare options in this chapter should at least give you an idea of the number of possible situations that exist, both at and away from home. To choose the situation that's right for you, you must consider your own values and priorities and the needs of your child, as well as the practical factors of cost and convenience.

Here's a quick review of the options we discussed:

- Care by a babysitter in your home—The child enjoys the security of her own home, but it may be difficult to find a qualified, long-term sitter.

- Care by a relative in your own home—The child feels secure at home, but it may prove difficult for the parents to stay in control and avoid personal conflicts.

- Care by a nanny in your own home—Nannies are qualified, dependable caregivers, but they are also full-time, live-in employees, making this the most expensive daycare option.

- Care by parents over staggered hours in their own home—It may be difficult for parents to set up complementary work schedules, but this option provides security for the child and saves the cost of alternative daycare.

- Care in a daycare center—The child is cared for by qualified individuals, but, depending on the center's policies and schedules, the arrangements may not always be convenient.

- Care in a daycare home—A daycare home offers a more homey atmosphere and accepts fewer children, but the mother is unlikely to be trained.

- Care in an infant care center—The needs of the infant child are well provided for, but because this idea is so new, it may be difficult to locate such a center.

- Care in a daycare center at work—At-work daycare is wonderfully convenient for the parents and employers; unfortunately, only very progressive (and usually large) employers provide this service.

Choosing daycare will be one of the first big decisions you make for you and your child. So take the time to research your options, review your own priorities, and sample what's available before you choose the daycare option that's right for your family. And after you've made a decision, keep on top of the situation. Your child is relying on you to provide good daycare.

Chapter 5

Handling Breast Milk: Pumping, Storing, and Transporting

Many employed, nursing mothers choose to leave breast milk, rather than formula, for their babies, for several reasons. For instance, the baby may be allergic or sensitive to formula, which is more common than many people realize. Or he may have some digestive difficulties. The mother may also feel that providing breast milk helps sustain the nurturing breastfeeding relationship. And she may not want her baby to miss the many nutritional benefits that breast milk provides.

Whatever her reason, the employed mother who chooses to leave breast milk will have to be organized and develop a routine for handling breast milk. In particular, she must learn how to pump the milk (either by hand expression or breast pump), how to store it, and how to transport it easily and safely.

Pumping

First, you need to decide how you will pump: by hand expression or by breast pump. If you choose to use a breast pump, you must also decide whether to use a manual pump, an electric pump, or a battery-operated pump. Some women rely completely on hand expression for their pumping, but most use a pump regularly and rely on hand expression only occasionally. Your hands are certainly more portable than a pump, but pumps are generally more effective.

Hand Expression

Many women prefer to use hand expression to pump their breast milk. It is an easy, convenient, and effective method of pumping, once you have mastered it. But in the beginning, you may find it awkward and slow.

We will present two methods of hand expression. Both methods work well. Try each and see which one is the most comfortable for you. Howevever, before you begin with either technique, wash your hands with soap. To store milk safely, it must be as bacteria free as possible. Pay careful attention to the cleanliness of your hands, as well as your collection and storage containers.

With any pumping method, you will find that switching breasts every few minutes will increase your effectiveness. This allows the milk to come down and collect in the sinuses of the breast that you aren't pumping. It may also help to hold the clean, glass container into which you are pumping between your legs and lean over it as you pump. This leaves both hands free to alternate pumping, and the effect of gravity should help, too. A two-cup glass measuring cup works well for this because of its wide mouth.

Technique 1. This technique was developed by long-time La Leche League leader Jo Ann Touchton, who has great expertise in the areas of hand expression and nursing problems.

1. Support your breast with the opposite hand (that is, left breast with right hand or vice versa), resting the heel of your palm against your ribs. Hold your first and second fingers apart, forming a V. Place these fingers on your breast, about 1½ inches back, one on either side of your nipple. This is where your lactiferous sinuses are. You may have to experiment and move either forward or backward from the nipple to obtain the best results.

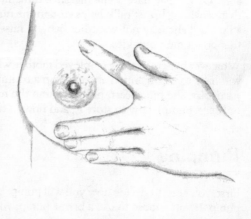

2. Squeeze your two fingers together and release a few times. Be sure to press them together like a pliers, so they meet straight and true; don't let your fingers cross over one another, like scissors. This squeezing should never feel like a pinch.

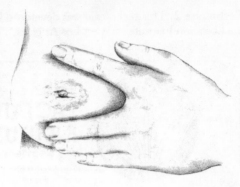

3. Rotate your hand to another point on the nipple, and repeat the process. Continue rotating, as if moving around a clock, until you have pumped all areas of the breast. Change hands when necessary to reach certain areas.

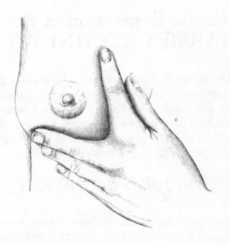

Once you have a feel for how much pressure you should use when squeezing with your two fingers (first and second), you can switch to using your thumb on the top and your middle finger on the bottom, since that seems a little easier. This method is much less awkward, but be careful: Don't use too much pressure or squeeze the whole breast with your hand. Doing so can cause pressure in a duct system and lead to breast infection.

If you don't seem to be getting much milk after a few minutes of hand expression, you may not be pumping at the right points. Try this technique (also developed by Jo Ann Touchton) for locating your lactiferous sinuses, which is where you should be pumping: Move your fingers backward from the tip of the nipple over the breast. At the tip and just behind the nipple, it feels like smooth tissue. About 1 to 1½ inches back, it feels like there are small lumps within the breast. These are the lactiferous sinuses. When you pump, your fingers should be just behind or on top of them.

Technique 2. This technique was developed by Chele Marmet, director of the Lactation Institute of West Los Angeles.*

THE LACTATION INSTITUTE
and Breastfeeding Clinic

® 16161 Ventura Blvd., Suite 223, Encino, CA 91436
(818) 995-1913

Manual Expression of Breast Milk
MARMET TECHNIQUE

The Marmet Technique of manual expression and assisting the milk ejection reflex (previously called the let-down reflex) has worked for hundreds of mothers— in a way that nothing has before. Even experienced breastfeeding mothers who have been able to hand express will find that this method produces more milk. Mothers who have previously been able to express only a small amount, or none at all, get excellent results with this technique.

TECHNIQUE IS IMPORTANT

When watching manual expression the correct milking motion is difficult to see. In this case the hand is quicker than the eye. Consequently, many mothers have found manual expression difficult—even after watching a demonstration or reading a brief description. Milk can be expressed when using less effective methods of hand expressions. When used, however, on a frequent and regular basis, these methods can easily lead to damaged breast tissue, bruised breasts, and even skin burns.

The Marmet technique of manual expresion was developed by a mother who needed to express her milk over an extended period of time for medical reasons. She found that her milk ejection reflex did not work as well as when her baby breastfed, so she also developed a method of massage and stimulation to assist this reflex. The key to the success of this technique is the combination of the method of expression and this massage.

---

*© 1978, revised 1979, 1981. Used with permission of Chele Marmet, The Lactation Institute and Breastfeeding Clinic, 16161 Ventura Blvd., Suite 223, Encino, California 91436, (818) 995-1913. Contact The Lactation Institute for bulk orders of this brochure.

This technique is effective and should not cause problems. It can easily be learned by following this step by step guide. As with any manual skill, practice is important.

ADVANTAGES

There are many advantages to manual expression over mechanical methods of milking the breasts:

• Some mechanical pumps cause discomfort and are ineffective.

• Many mothers are more comfortable with manual expression of breast milk because it is more natural.

• Skin-to-skin contact is more stimulating than the feel of a plastic shield. So manual expression usually allows for an easier milk ejection reflex.

• It's convenient.

• It's ecologically superior.

• It's portable. How can a mother forget her hands?

• Best of all it's free!

HOW THE BREAST WORKS

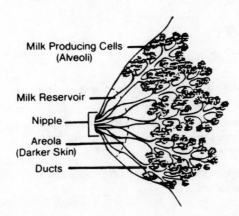

The milk is produced in milk producing cells (alveoli). A portion of the milk continuously comes down the ducts and collects in the milk reservoirs. When the milk-producing cells are stimulated, they expel additional milk into the duct system (milk ejection reflex).

EXPRESSING THE MILK
Draining The Milk Reservoirs

1. POSITION the thumb and first two fingers about **1" to 1½" behind the nipple.** Be sure the hand forms the letter "c" and finger pads are at 12 and 6 o'clock in line with the nipple.

• Use this measurement, which is not necessarily the outer edge of the areola, as a guide. The areola varies in size from one woman to another.

• Place the thumb above the nipple and the fingers below as shown.

• Note that the fingers are positioned so that the milk reservoirs lie beneath them.

• Avoid cupping the breast.

2. PUSH straight into the chest wall.
• Avoid spreading the fingers apart.

• For large breasts, first lift and then push into the chest wall.

Push into Chest Wall

3. ROLL thumb and fingers forward as if making thumb and fingerprints at the same time.

• The **rolling motion** of the thumb and fingers compresses and empties the milk reservoirs without hurting sensitive breast tissue.

• Note the moving position of the thumbnail and fingernails in illustration.

Roll

Finish Roll

4. REPEAT RHYTHMICALLY to drain the reservoirs.

• Position, push, roll; position, push, roll . . .

5. ROTATE the thumb and finger position to milk the other reservoirs. Use both hands on each breast. These pictures show hand positions on the right breast.

Right Hand   **Left Hand**

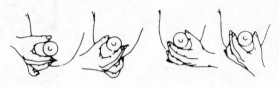

AVOID THESE MOTIONS

Avoid squeezing the breast. This can cause bruising.

Avoid pulling out the nipple and breast. This can cause tissue damage.

Avoid sliding on the breast. This can cause skin burns.

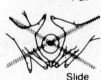

Squeeze

Pull

Slide

ASSISTING THE MILK EJECTION REFLEX
Stimulating The Flow Of Milk

1. MASSAGE the milk producing cells and ducts.

• Start at the top of the breast. Press firmly into the chest wall. Move fingers in a circular motion on one spot on the skin.

MASSAGE

- After a few seconds move the fingers to the next area on the breast.
- **Spiral** around the breast toward the areola using this massage.
- The motion is similar to that used in a breast examination.

2. **STROKE** the breast area from the top of the breast to the nipple with a light **tickle-like stroke.**

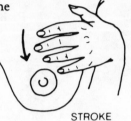

STROKE

- Continue this stroking motion from the chest wall to the nipple around the whole breast.
- This will help with relaxation and will help stimulate the milk ejection reflex.

3. **SHAKE** the breast while leaning forward so that gravity will help the milk eject.

SHAKE

PROCEDURE

This procedure should be followed by mothers who are expressing in place of a full feeding and those who need to establish, increase, or maintain their milk supply when the baby cannot breastfeed.

- Express each breast until the flow of milk slows down.
- Assist the milk ejection reflex (massage, stroke, shake) on both breasts. This can be done simultaneously.
- Repeat the whole process of expressing each breast and assisting the milk ejection reflex once or twice more. The flow of milk usually slows down sooner the second and third time as the reservoirs are drained.

TIMING

The **ENTIRE PROCEDURE** should take approximately **20–30 MINUTES.**

- Express each breast 5–7 minutes.
- Massage, stroke, shake.
- Express each breast 3–5 minutes.
- Massage, stroke, shake.
- Express each breast 2–3 minutes.

Note: If the milk supply is established, use the times given only as a guide. Watch the flow of milk and change breasts when the flow gets small.

Note: If little or no milk is present yet, follow these suggested times closely.

© 1978, revised 1979, 1981. Used with permission of Chele Marmet, The Lactation Institute and Breastfeeding Clinic, 16161 Ventura Blvd., Suite 223, Encino, California 91436.

Breast Pumps

Many women use hand expression exclusively to pump milk; this may be especially suitable for the mother who only works part-time. But hand expression is not practical for all nursing mothers, especially those who are employed full-time and may have other outside activites. Most employed women are more satisifed using a breast pump, which is faster and more efficient than hand expressing.

All breast pumps operate on the same principle: A vacuum is created while a breast shield in in place, and the milk is drawn out and flows into a collection vessel or bottle. There are manual pumps, battery pumps, and electric pumps, ranging in price from $5.00 to $1,000 dollars. We will discuss the types of pumps, as well as specific models, in Chapter 6, "Selecting a Breast Pump."

Other Considerations

When to Pump. You will need to determine how often you need to or are able to pump at work. Some women find that it works best to pump at about the same time the baby would be nursing if she were at home, since your milk supply is already geared toward that schedule. If you can't pump at that time, don't worry. Your fullest periods will soon readjust to coincide with your pumping times.

Marilyn, an educational consultant we talked to, told us, "I find that to get a letdown consistently and keep my supply up, I need to pump at the same time my baby would normally nurse."

However, other mothers find that their letdowns can be easily programmed to the new routine of breaks and lunchtime. Some pump twice a day, at lunch and at break, while others pump only once, at lunch. How often you have to pump will be determined by two things: (1) how much milk you can get at each pumping and (2) how flexible your work schedule is.

For example, Terri, another mother, pumps eight ounces of breast milk a day. She says, "I found that I had the most milk in the morning and late at night. So I pumped about two ounces right after his first nursing in the morning, four ounces on my lunch hour, and two more ounces just before bed."

One of the most important things to know before you pump: In the beginning, you may get very little milk when you pump. In fact, when you are just learning, you may get less than an ounce at a time. But don't get discouraged, and keep trying. You'll become more and more proficient as you go—some women eventually get as much as eight ounces at one sitting.

How Long to Pump. A pumping will usually take around twenty minutes. This varies significantly, of course, depending on how much milk you need to pump. If your goal is two ounces, it may take less time. Some women need 30 minutes for larger amounts. How much milk you get in a given amount of time is extremely individual.

If you alternate breasts frequently, you will probably get more milk, since the milk on the side you're not pumping is draining down into the lactiferous sinuses and will be pumped out easily.

Achieving Letdown. In order to get your milk out effectively, you must have a letdown. Remember, while some women feel a tingling or even a mild ache, others never feel any particular sensation when they letdown. But you do not need to **feel** one to **have** one.

If you have trouble getting a letdown, try stimulating your nipple before you pump. One mother, a nurse practitioner, wets her fingers with warm water and pulls gently on her nipples to aid the letdown. Doing so probably creates a feeling similar to that of her baby's mouth on her breast.

It is also helpful to be able to pump in a quiet place where you are comfortable enough to relax. Your mental set is important, so take a moment to get out of your "employee" frame of mind and into your "mother" frame of mind. Try your childbirth education relaxation techniques for a minute or two. Then think of your baby—how he looks, how he feels, how he smells and sounds. Some women even look at a picture of the baby while they pump. And one woman looks at a picture of herself nursing her baby!

A woman who has severe problems with letdown can ask her doctor to prescribe Syntocinin, an artificial oxytocin, which is the letdown hormone. Syntocinin comes in a nasal spray form and will help to induce a letdown. Many women are successful with only half a dose. But do try other methods first, and use Syntocinin only as a last resort. Repeated use is not recommended because it can cause a rebound effect, defeating its purpose.

Some women who have high-pressured jobs simply cannot achieve a letdown at work. If this happens to you, don't feel that you need to give up nursing. Compromise. Nurse when you're with your baby, and leave formula for him when you're at work.

Pumping at Home. While many women pump only at work, some women feel they cannot meet their baby's requirements if they don't pump at home, too. But some women take this concern too far. When they pump at home, they pump immediately **before** they nurse the baby, because they are so concerned about getting enough milk for the bottle. Doing so creates an unfortunate competition: Nursing on a partially empty breast is frustrating and unsatisfying for the baby. On the other hand, feeding from a bottle is easy and fulfilling. It is no wonder that, when faced with such a choice, the baby will soon choose the bottle.

Clearly, pumping to fill a bottle before you nurse defeats your original intention. Do you want your baby to enjoy a pleasurable, satisfying experience at the breast, perhaps supplementing his needs with formula occasionally? Or do you want to make nursing difficult and frustrating, causing him to prefer bottlefeeding over breastfeeding? Reassure yourself once in awhile and remember that the mothering you do is almost always more important than the substance you put into your baby's stomach. So if you need to pump at home, do. But nurse your baby **first.**

Taking Care of Yourself. For your own health and well-being—and also to maintain a good milk supply—you need to take care of yourself, as well as your baby. Keep high-protein and nutritious snacks, like nuts or dried fruit, where they are easily accessible: in your car, in your purse, and at your desk. You may also want to take a good vitamin supplement. Or try making a high-protein drink to have for breakfast or take along to work in a thermos. Keep up your fluid intake while you're working.

As difficult as it may be, try to get as much extra rest as you can. Go to bed as early as possible. You can minimize lost sleep by bringing the baby into your bed for night nursings and just going back to sleep with him. (No, you won't roll over on him!) Napping with the baby on weekends and days off is another good idea. Overall, try not to overload yourself during this time.

Wardrobe. If you intend to pump at work, you must wear appropriate clothing. Basically, you need either two-piece outfits (a top with a skirt or pants) or something that buttons in front (a top or dress). With a little experimentation, you will surely find enough outfits that facilitate pumping yet are appropriate for work.

Avoid dresses or blouses that zip or button in the back, since they must be taken completely off in order to nurse or pump. Outfits that have a blouse and a jacket are usually your best choice; they are both conveneint for pumping and businesslike in appearance. (See also the discussion of clothing in Chapter 3, "Your Wardrobe," p. 47.)

When Pumping Ends. Remember, even though you may not wean for some time, you may reach a point where you will either no longer need to pump at work or you will become less eager to continue. This is likely to happen after your baby is six months old or so, when he will probably be drinking juice and eating a significant amount of food. At this time, you may feel that you don't need to supply breast milk for the baby while he's at the sitter's. Or you may feel that one bottle, which you can supply by pumping at home, is sufficient.

Your feelings may also change during the course of your nursing relationship. In the beginning, you will probably feel very committed to pumping your milk at work, partly because it helps you feel that you are mothering your baby during that time. At some later point, as you recognize that your baby's physical need for breast milk is lessening, you may feel your own social needs becoming more important. For instance, you may begin to miss having lunch with your peers and choose to forego pumping at that time.

We won't offer you a timetable, stating how long you should continue pumping during your lunch at work every day. Instead, we recommend that you let your perception of your and your baby's needs be your guide.

Storing

If you are going to store breast milk, you need to learn some basic facts about how to store it safely. Remember: Breast milk contains some bacteria from your skin, which can multiply if not stored properly. If you accidentally give your baby spoiled breast milk, he may end up vomiting and having diarrhea.

Cleanliness

As we mentioned in the section on hand-expressing, your first step should be to wash your hands thoroughly with soap. If you are using a breast pump, make sure it is clean before you begin. Follow the directions with the pump for advice on proper cleaning. Finally, make sure your collection container is clean, too.

It's also important that the bottles you use to store the milk are clean. If you have a dishwasher, use it; otherwise, hot water and soap will do. If you want to sterilize the bottles, the water in your dishwasher must reach 180° F., or you must boil them for twenty to twenty-five minutes. Most doctors no longer recommend sterilization.

Freezing and Refrigerating Milk

After you pump your milk into a clean container, pour it into the bottle. If you are going to add fresh milk to previously frozen milk, keep the fresh milk in the back of the refrigerator, covered, to cool for half an hour before pouring in on top of the frozen milk. If you were to pour warm milk on top of frozen milk, the top of the frozen layer would defrost and then refreeze. **Breast milk should never be refrozen.**

When you freeze milk in layers like this, new and old, you will be able to see the different layers. This is normal. The color will vary according to the fat content of the milk.

If you will use freshly pumped milk within 48 hours, you can keep it in the refrigerator. If you won't use it that soon, freeze it, and mark the date on the bottle. Always use the oldest milk first. You can pour cooled fresh milk into a bottle of older milk to make the number of ounces you need, but if you mix new milk with old, go by the old date. Breast milk can be frozen if it has been refrigerated 24 hours or less. **Do not freeze milk that has been stored for more than 24 hours.**

A nurse in Denver came up with a creative idea: She froze milk in plastic ice cube trays. Each cube equalled about one ounce of milk. Once the cubes were frozen, she popped them out of the tray, placed them in a plastic bag, and dated the package. She kept the bag of cubes at the babysitter's, which worked out well. If her son was not quite satisfied with his feeding or if he became hungry before she returned from work, milk was available in small quantities, so he could be fed without defrosting an entire new bottle of milk. We must point out that this mother followed appropriate cleanliness practices throughout the process. She was careful that the milk in a single tray was pumped at about the same time, and she was sure not to pour warm milk on top of frozen. She also covered the tray during freezing, and the cubes were stored in an airtight plastic bag.

How long can you store frozen breast milk? The colder the freezer stays, the longer milk will last. In an old-fashioned, small freezer compartment within the refrigerator, breast milk will last only three weeks. But in most modern units, which have a separate door or compartment for the freezer (above, below, or alongside the regular refrigerator section), breast milk will last three months. To check on how well your frozen milk is keeping, try the ice cream test: If ice cream stays good and hard in your freezer, breast milk should last three months. In a deep freeze that stays below 0° F. and is rarely opened, milk will last six months to a year.

Once breast milk is thawed, it can be kept in the refrigerator and used up to 24 hours later. **Again, don't keep thawed milk for longer than 24 hours.**

The best routine is to give the baby the fresh milk you pump on the following day, and use frozen milk only if you need a supplement. For when breast milk is frozen, some of the antibodies and nutrients it contains are destroyed and will thus not be absorbed the baby. But don't let this worry you if only a small amount of your baby's feedings consist of frozen breast milk. After all, formula doesn't contain any antibodies.

Thawing

After you have followed the right steps to pump and store your breast milk, be sure to give your babysitter very specific instructions for thawing and warming the stored milk. This is very important.

If the milk you provide is fresh, the babysitter must keep it in the refrigerator until just before she uses it. When she warms it, she should either do it under warm, running tap water or in a pan of water on the stove. She should not overheat it. Also advise her never to set the bottle out at room temperature to warm. Breast milk cannot be unrefrigerated that long.

If you give the babysitter frozen milk, she should not set it out to thaw. To thaw the milk, she should hold the bottle under cool, running tap water, gradually increasing the temperature from cool to tepid to warm. She can continue to warm the bottle under the tap water, or, once the milk is all liquid, she can heat it in a pan of water on the stove. Instruct her never to thaw frozen breast milk in a pan on the stove. Doing so will curdle the milk and make it undrinkable.

We also caution against thawing or heating breast milk in a microwave oven. Besides the possible danger of getting the milk too hot, the microwave process may affect the nutrients in the milk.

Again, once a bottle of frozen milk has been thawed, it will stay good in the refrigerator for only 24 hours. If the baby does not finish a bottle during that time, discard it.

Times to Remember

Next feeding	The bottle of breast milk that was offered at the previous feeding can be used.
30 minutes	Cool fresh breast milk in the refrigerator before adding it to previously frozen milk.
1 hour	Thawed or fresh breast milk can remain at room temperature.
24 hours	Thawed, frozen breast milk is safe, if kept refrigerated.
24 hours	Fresh breast milk can be refrigerated and then frozen.
48 hours	Fresh breast milk can be refrigerated and then used.
3 weeks	Frozen breast milk is safe in a small freezer section within the refrigerator.
3 months	Frozen breast milk is safe in a separate freezer compartment of the refrigerator.
6 months to 1 year	Frozen breast milk is safe if in a deepfreeze that stays at 0° F. or below, like a chest freezer.

Storing at Work

When you pump your milk at work, be very careful as to how you store it. It must be **cooled immediately** and **kept cool** consistently thereafter.

Some women take a small cooler to work for this purpose and precool it with ice cubes or blue ice packs. The type of cooler that is designed to use blue ice in the lid is probably the most convenient.

If you can, find a refrigerator you can use at work, since this is the simplest storage solution. Unfortunately, not all employees have that luxury. If a refrigerator is not already available, consider buying a small one or starting an employee pool to buy one, if your co-workers seem eager to participate. After all, refrigerators can be used for other things than storing breast milk!

A Word of Caution

You may have considered wearing plastic breast shields at work and saving the milk that leaks into them. Don't do it. It is not safe to use breast milk that has been stored at room temperature or body temperature, since bacteria thrives in a warm environment. You could end up making your baby sick by giving him spoiled milk.

Transporting

Since your chilled or frozen breast milk must be kept cool during transit, the key to transporting breast milk is to do so as little as possible. This will make life easier for you and will also reduce the possibility of spoilage.

The best arrangement is drop breast milk off at the babysitter's the same day that you pump it, so it can be used fresh the next day. For instance, bring it right from work when you pick up your baby at night. If you need to freeze it, do so at the babysitter's house. (Remember to date it.)

The best means of transporting milk to your home or the babysitter's is an insulated bottle bag. They are inexpensive and can be purchased in a baby goods store. You can also transport frozen milk this way, using bags or bottles. We placed a bottle of frozen milk in one of these bags and it was still frozen solid three hours later. Try this experiment with your own bag, since different bags may be more or less efficient. If you transport refrigerated milk, be sure to verify that the bag still feels really cold when you arrive at your destination.

You can also use an ice chest to transport milk fresh or frozen milk. The most convenient type is a small one that has blue ice built into the lid. If you freeze the lid each night, it will be ready to use the next morning. Of course, you can use any ice chest with frozen blue ice. Regular ice will probably not stay frozen as long and you will end up with a lot of water in your chest. It will also be inconvenient to make enough ice every day.

Whatever means you choose to use, if you transport frozen milk, it must stay completely frozen. Thawing may lead to refreezing, which must always be avoided. If you should discover that your milk has begun to thaw, finish thawing it under running water and use it within 24 hours. Or else throw it away. Do not refreeze it.

Summary

Once you know the safety factors involved and develop regular steps for pumping, storing, and transporting milk, this routine will become a natural part of your life. The most important thing is that you develop good habits from the start. If you don't, you will run the risk of feeding your baby contaminated milk.

Whether you use hand expression or a breast pump, follow these basic guidelines for pumping:

• Before you begin, wash your hands thoroughly and make sure your collection and storage containers are clean.

• Switch breasts every few minutes to increase your effectiveness.

• Determine how often you need to pump based on how much milk you get at each pumping and how flexible your work schedule is.

• When you pump at work, try to find a relaxing, comfortable place and use any other helpful techniques to help achieve a letdown.

• If you pump at home, be sure to nurse your baby first and pump second.

• For your own well-being and to maintain an adequate milk supply, take care of yourself by eating properly and getting enough rest.

• Rely on your own perception of your and your baby's needs to determine when to pump less or stop completely.

We cannot overemphasize the need for safe and clean storage of breast milk. In particular, remember these "nevers:"

• **Never** store fresh milk in the refrigerator for more than 48 hours.

• **Never** freeze milk that has been stored for more than 24 hours.

• **Never** thaw frozen breast milk by letting it stand at room temperature.

• **Never** heat breast milk unless it is first completely thawed and in liquid form.

• **Never** refreeze breast milk once it has begun to thaw.

A final word of caution: Should you ever suspect that a bottle of milk is too old, has set out too long, or has been allowed to thaw and refreeze, discard it. Yes, it hurts to see your hard work literally go down the drain, but you don't want to risk feeding contaminated milk to your baby.

Chapter 6

Selecting a Breast Pump

If you plan to use a breast pump, you need to look into the various types of pumps that are available and decide which is right for you. You'll want to look for one that is affordable and easy to use, transport, and clean. But be forewarned: You will undoubtedly be surprised at the number and variety of pumps that you'll find.

We'll help you sort it all out in this chapter. We'll discuss the three basic types of pumps—manual, electric, and battery-operated—and provide operational, convenience, and cost details about a number of the specific models available.

Manual Pumps

Every pump requires some type of power to create the negative pressure—or suction—that will draw the milk out of the breast. Manual pumps are simply powered by something the user does.

Most manual pumps are small, lightweight, and easy to transport. They are also generally less expensive than most electric pumps. Many employed mothers find that a manual pump is adequate for their needs.

Brands of Manual Pumps

• LePump Breast Feeding System, Labtron Scientific Corporation, 91 Cabot Court, Hauppauge, NY 11788

LePump is a manual pump that operates on a very simple principle: The breast shield and a tube with a suction bulb are screwed onto a baby bottle; squeezing and releasing the bulb creates suction to draw the milk out, and it flows directly into the bottle. The suction pressure can be increased or decreased by twisting the lid of the bottle.

Some women say that this type of pumping is less tiring than other manual methods. This pump also comes with adaptors for small- or medium-sized breasts. It costs about $18.00.

• Ora'Lac, Ora'Lac Pump, Inc., Division of Lunas Enterprises, Box 2400, Sitka, AK 99835

The Ora'Lac breast pump was designed by a nursing mother and uses a different source of power from any other pump. Two tubes extend from the collecting bottle: one connects to the breast shield and one goes to the mother's mouth. The mother's gentle suction on this tube creates the vacuum that draws the milk out.

This small pump fits in a purse, and, unlike other pumps, it can be used while the mother is lying down. This pump costs about $30.00.

• The Medela Manualectric Breast Pump/Feeding System, Medela, Inc., P.O. Box 386, Crystal Lake, IL 60014

The Medela hand pump is designed around the suck/release/relax cycle of a baby's nursing pattern. It uses a piston-type pumping action; the vacuum is automatically released through vents at the end of each suction stroke. The milk goes directly into an attached bottle.

The pump system includes an adapter for small or large breasts and an adapter kit for an electric breast pump. And since a kit must be purchased in order to use any electric pump, this is ideal for a woman who may also need to use an electric pump (see the following section, "Electric Pumps"). Any standard baby bottle may be used. The total cost of the system is about $25.00.

• Loyd-B Pump, Lopuco, Ltd., 1615 Old Annapolis Road, Woodbine, MD 21797

The Loyd-B operates through a trigger mechanism, much like those on spray bottles. Pulling the trigger causes suction, and the milk flows into an attached glass jar.

The Loyd-B is a little more bulky than some manual pumps, but it comes apart easily and is small enough to carry in your purse. It was one of the first manual pumps made, and many women continue to use it successfully. The cost of the Loyd-B is about $40.00.

Cylinder Pumps

By far, the most popular type of manual pump is the cylinder pump. While there are many, many brands, they all operate in the same basic way: Two concentric cylinders, one slightly smaller than the other, fit together and are

The Loyd-B Manual Pump

The Loyd-B manual pump operates through a basic trigger mechanism, squeezing the handle to the grip on the right, much like a spray bottle. This was one of the first pumps made, and many women continue to use it successfully.

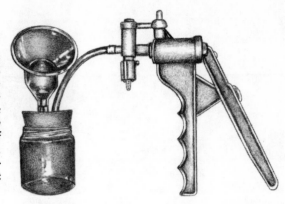

joined with a gasket seal. One cylinder has a breast flange at one end; when it is placed against the breast, suction is created by drawing the large cylinder outward in a pistonlike motion. The large cylinder collects the milk and can usually double as a bottle when the inner cylinder is removed and a nipple is attached.

Cylinder pumps are easy to use and can be cleaned in the dishwasher. They are small, lightweight, and can be taken to and from work easily. Most cylinder pumps come with two adapters for varying breast size.

Many brands of cylinder pumps are on the market, including the following:

- the au natural Breastfeeding System
- the AXi-pump
- the Comfort Plus Deluxe Breast Pump (by Kaneson)
- the Egnell Hand Breast Pump-Infant Nursing System
- the Evenflo Natural Mother Deluxe Breastfeeding Set
- the Faultless Breast Pump
- the Infa Complete Breast Pump and Milk Storage System (by Monterey Labs)
- the Nuk Breast Pump Kit (by Reliance Products)
- the Nursing Mother Breast Pump Kit (by Mary Jane)
- the Precious Care by Gerber

All of these pumps are fairly similar and can be found in most baby stores and many department and drug stores. Cylinder pumps range in price from $15.00 to $23.00. For more information on individual models, contact the companies listed below:

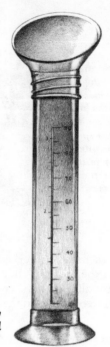

A Cylinder-type Manual Pump

The cylinder-type manual pump is very popular. It is effective, easy to use, and small enough to carry in your purse.

- Ameda/Egnell, 765 Industrial Drive, Cary, IL 60013

- au natural, Healthmed, Inc., P.O. Box 6448, Edison, NJ 08818

- AXicare Pumps, D. J. Colgate Medical Ltd., Chanin Building, 17th Floor, 122 East 42nd Street, New York, NY 10168

- Evenflo Products Co., 771 North Freedom Street, P.O. Box 190, Ravenna, OH 44266

- Faultless Breast Pump, Ross Laboratories, Division of Abbott Laboratories, 625 Cleveland, Columbus, OH 43216

- Gerber Products Co., 445 State Street, Fremont, MI 49412

- Infa, Monterey Laboratories, Inc., P.O. Box 15129, Las Vegas, NV 89114

- Kaneson, Marshall Electronics, Inc., 600 Barclay Blvd., Lincolnshire, IL 60069

- Mary Jane Pumps, The Mary Jane Company, 5510 Cleon Avenue, North Hollywood, CA 91609

- Nuk, Reliance Products Corporation, 108 Mason Street, Woonsocket, RI 02895

Electric Pumps

While most women use a manual breast pump, you may want to investigate the ease and convenience of an electric pump before you make your selection. Electric pumps operate through a motor-driven suction (something like a vacuum cleaner) that alternates sucking and releasing to simulate the suction rhythm of a nursing baby.

In addition to being the easiest way to pump breast milk, an electric pump will also empty your breasts more thoroughly than a manual pump. For this reason, an electric pump may be more effective in helping you maintain an adequate milk supply.

Electric pumps range in price from $29.00 to $1,000.00. The larger, full-size models may be rented from many pharmacies and most medical-supply outlets. Renting will cost approximately $60.00 per month, plus $10.00 to $15.00 for the one-time purchase of a starter kit containing bottles and tubing. Discounted long-term rental rates may be available, so be sure to check around. If your doctor prescribes use of an electric pump for a valid medical reason, your health insurance may cover at least part of the cost of renting.

Brands of Electric Pumps

• Egnell Electric Breast Pump, Ameda/Egnell, 765 Industrial Drive, Cary, IL 60013

• Medela Electric Pump, Medela, Inc., P.O. Box 386, Crystal Lake, IL 60014

Two of the most popular full-size models, which are usually found in hospitals, are the Egnell Electric Breast Pump and the Medela Electric Pump. Both pumps operate through alternating suction, which imitates a baby's sucking. Both pumps also have an adjustable suction control and are very easy to operate. A word of caution: Read the instructions that accompany the pump, and be careful until you are familiar with the pump and how much suction it creates.

Although the two pumps are very similar, the Medela is a little smaller and lighter than the Egnell. Still, both pumps are roughly the same size and weight as a small portable sewing machine. Although it may not be easy to transport an electric pump back and forth from work, it is possible. Or you may prefer to leave the pump at work and only use it there.

Since both the Egnell and Medela pumps cost almost $1,000.00, rental is an obvious option. Call local medical rental facilities or pharmacies to find a breast pump rental outlet. If you can't find one, try writing to the companies for the outlet nearest you (addresses given above). The rental fee for both pumps will probably be about the same.

An Electric Pump

The employed mother may want to consider buying or renting an electric pump. It is the easiest method of pumping and the most efficient, as well.

• The Mary Jane Electric Pump, The Mary Jane Company, Designer Series, 5510 Cleon Avenue, North Hollywood, CA 91609

The new Mary Jane Electric Pump is a midsize electric pump. The design of this pump shows careful planning: It uses an overflow bottle to prevent milk from backing up into the pump, as well as a mechanism that shuts the pump off automatically if it becomes overheated. The Mary Jane has an on/off switch, and you can control the pump's suction with your finger.

The safety features, size, and price (about $175.00) of this pump make it a good model for a breastfeeding mother who works full-time.

• AXicare Pumps, D. J. Colgate Medical Ltd., Chanin Building, 17th Floor, 122 East 42nd Street, New York, NY 10168

AXicare manufacturers a variety of breast pumps. The CM14 is the largest fully automatic electric pump. Another fully automatic pump, the CM10, is portable and regulates suction and relaxation with an adjustable vacuum scale. The CM8 is a semiautomatic model that allows users to regulate suction.

The CM10 and the CM8 are about the size of a lunch box. All three of these pumps are available for rental.

AXicare also makes two smaller, less expensive electric pumps. The CM4 Mini Breast Pump is semiautomatic, like the CM8, but it is small enough to fit in a handbag. (It does not come with a carrying case.) Women who use it report that it's very effective. It retails for about $89.00

• Gerber Precious Care Electric Breast Pump Kit, Gerber Products Co., 445 State Street, Fremont, MI 49412

The smallest and least expensive nonbattery electric breast pump, the Gerber Precious Care, is another good choice for an employed, nursing mother. This pump is lightweight, quiet, and has an on/off switch. The breast milk is pumped directly into a baby bottle. All of the parts (except the pump itself) are boilable.

The kit includes a 4-ounce bottle, a Nuk nipple, and a cleaning brush. It costs about $50.00

• White River Electric Breast Pump, Natural Technologies, Inc., P.O. Box 1704, Beaverton, OR 97005

The White River electric breast pump offers a unique feature that boasts great benefits: It is the only pump with a soft, flexible flange (the cupped part that goes over the breast). This flexibility provides for a more thorough emptying and raises the mother's prolactin level by compressing the areola and nipple during pumping, rather than just extracting the milk.

White River pumps come in relatively small carrying cases, weighing a total of less than 10 pounds. They are available for rental at many medical outlets.

Battery-operated Pumps

Battery-operated pumps are the newest concept in breast pumps. They have two main advantages: They are small and they do not require that the user be near an electrical outlet. Thus, they are very convenient and portable. The disadvantage of battery-operated pumps is the cost of the batteries, which could be significant; this cost could be reduced by using recharageable batteries.

• The Gentle Expressions Automatic Breast Pump and Feeding System, Healthteam/Division of M. E. Team, Inc., 625 Montrose Avenue, South Plainfield, NJ 07080

The Gentle Expressions Automatic Breast Pump and Feeding System operates on two AA batteries. This pump is small, lightweight (10 ounces), and has high- or low-volume control. The suction release valve is operated by your fingertip, and the milk is pumped directly from the breast shield into a baby bottle.

Although this pump doesn't have the suction power of the larger pumps, it only costs about $30.00, making it a worthwhile investment.

• The MagMag Battery-operated Breast Pump and Training Cup System, Marshall Baby Care Products, Division of Marshall Electronics, Inc., 600 Barclay Blvd., Lincolnshire, IL 60060

The MagMag—another of the new, small and lightweight battery-operated pumps—comes with a four-step cup system, designed to help teach a child to drink from a cup. The MagMag pump also screws directly onto a standard baby bottle.

The MagMag is dishwasher safe, which is very convenient. And it is inexpensive, costing about $39.00.

Summary

Certainly, not all mothers who nurse will want or need to pump. But for the mother who works, whether full- or part-time, pumping will probably be a very routine part of her breastfeeding.

As you decide which pump to use, consider the following:

• How much does it cost? Should I buy a pump or rent one? Will my insurance cover any of the cost?

• How portable is it? Can I take the pump apart and carry it in my purse or a small bag? Or will it be easier to leave it at the office?

• How efficient is it? How long will it take me to pump?

• How easy is it to use? Does the pump have adapters for different breast sizes? Can the suction and power be adjusted easily? Are there any cautions for use?

• How easy will it be to clean? Can the separate pieces of the pump go in the dishwasher or be boiled? Does it have any special cleaning features?

And once you've decided on the pump for you, be sure to read all of the directions that come with it, particularly if you've chosen an electric or battery-operated pump.

Chapter 7

Working It Out at Work

Should I rearrange my schedule? How much leave do I need? Where is the best place to pump? When is the best time? Do I have to tell my boss about what I'm doing?

These are the questions that many employed, breastfeeding mothers ask. And this is an area in which we don't have all the answers. The solutions to the logistics of breastfeeding when employed are as numerous and varied as the women who choose to nurse and work.

Your own solution will depend entirely on your individual situation. And you are the best judge of that. Thus, it seems that those women who are able to accept that there is no standard, no "right answer," and who assume full responsibility for creating their own workable plan are the most successful in combining working and breastfeeding.

Although we cannot give all-purpose advice, we can offer some things to think about and share what other women have discovered. That's the purpose of this chapter. The rest is up to you.

Maternity Leave

Don't underestimate the magnitude of the adjustments you'll face as a new parent. Rare is the woman whose experience matches the standard expectation that "I'll soon be bored at home because babies sleep so much, and after a week or two we'll get used to dropping the baby off at the sitter's on the way to work." Always plan for the outside limit. Then let yourself be pleasantly surprised if things go smoothly.

The standard six-week maternity leave is just barely enough for most women. Most mothers plan to do much more with their six weeks of perceived leisure than is realistic, so they are disappointed to find that their leave time doesn't meet any of their expectations. Besides, jumping back into work full-time is very hard after just having had a baby.

Plan to take as much leave time as you can possibly afford and your company will allow. And then erase your mental picture of a vacationlike period of bliss with your new baby. We don't want to make things sound too bleak, but most women find their maternity leave to be very short and very stressful. So lower your expectations somewhat, and prepare to face reality. Then, should your leave be blissful after all, you can say we misadvised you!

If at all possible, ease back into your work schedule. Maybe you can work part-time or reduce hours for awhile until you're ready to go back full-time. But beware: One new mother arranged to work a few days a week and ended up putting in forty hours in three days instead of five! Also see if you can avoid any extra duties and travel for awhile.

Deciding how and when to return to work after having a baby poses a real dilemma: On the one hand, you want to keep your needs as a new mother in mind, planning a schedule that is as easy and gradual as possible. On the other hand, you undoubtedly want to maintain your image as a competent employee, capable of stepping right back in without missing a beat. As with anything involving the unknown, plan for the less-than-best case. If you end up doing more, sooner than you expected, great. (See the section of planning your maternity leave, "Your Work," in Chapter 3.)

Working around
Your Work Schedule

Another work-related concern is pumping: when, where, and how? As you try to plan a routine, keep these general guidelines in mind:

• Women who work eight-hour days are away from their baby nine to ten hours, counting lunch and travel time. During this time, most women need to pump two to three times to maintain their supply, possibly in addition to pumping again at home.

• A pumping will usually take 20 to 30 minutes, when you include preparation, pumping, and clean up. Still, some women do manage on a standard 15-minute break. If you ever find yourself with only a short amount of time, pump anyway. Even if you do not "finish," you will relieve at least some of the pressure and fullness, which will help you last until your next pumping.

• The best possible work schedule is one that allows for flexible breaks and lunch times. Then, you can take a pumping break for as long as you need, subtracting that time from your lunch or break or adding it at the start or end of the day. However, many women with set lunch and break times manage to pump with no problems at all.

• Expect supply ups and downs. For instance, you may notice that your afternoon pumpings yield less milk than those earlier in the day, and by Thursday or Friday (if you work a standard week), you might have less milk than you did earlier in the week. This is normal. A weekend of plentiful nursing will bring your supply right back up.

Nine to Five

If you work regular, daytime hours, with a lunch hour and two breaks, you have few choices about planning when to pump. Most women find that they need a minimum of 20 minutes to pump; 30 minutes is a little more realistic. The woman on a nine-to-five schedule will have to plan carefully:

• Pump before work, in the evening, and once over your lunch hour, **or**

• Pump before and after work and twice during the day. You may be able to take care of pumping over your two breaks and keep your lunch hour free, or you may need to take two half-hour breaks and only a half-hour lunch. One woman on a strict schedule could take only her half-hour lunch and two 15-minute breaks. She arranged to take 20 minutes for each break and 20 minutes for lunch, so she could manage two pumpings a day, **or**

• Give your baby formula while you are at work and continue to breastfeed when you are at home. Many babies adjust to this routine quite nicely, as long as Mother is not the one offering the formula. Your milk supply is amazingly adaptable. If you don't pump the excess milk when you are at work, you will simply have less milk during the hours that you work and more when you are home. (You will go through an adjustment period while your body adapts to the new schedule.) Even the differing demands of weekends don't seem to be a big problem for women who have adjusted to such a schedule.

If your schedule is more erratic, you may have more difficulty planning when to pump. Most women find that it is better to pump when they become full, rather than having to wait and plan pumping around meetings and the like.

Part-timers

Part-time is always easier than full-time, no matter what sort of schedule you have. If you work four or five days of short shifts, you may only have to pump once per shift. Or you could probably pump only at home and have enough milk to make up the one feeding a day that you might miss. The proportion of nursings at home would stabilize your supply.

If you work two or three full days a week, follow the guidelines for working full-time.

Working at Home

Working at home provides a wonderful situation. You are right there, at home, with your baby, so you don't need to pump and transport milk all over town. And you are in charge of your own schedule, so you don't face the conflicts of keeping an employer happy. If you need to set up meetings or errands, do so with your nursing schedule in mind, and you will probably be able to avoid pumping altogether.

The most common drawback of this arrangement is the potential psychological conflict created by having no separation between "work time" and "mother time." To deal with this "mixed bag," you will need to accept that, as a full-time mother, you will accomplish less in a day of work than you did before. Keep the advantages in mind: Working at home can be the ideal breastfeeding situation. (See also the sections "Working Freelance" and "Working at Home" in Chapter 8.)

School Days

The mother who is in school may find that being a full-time student coincides nicely with being a nursing mother. Campus protocol is so much less stringent than that of most employment situations that you can usually work out any plan that suits you. For instance, many parents alternate taking baby to classes in a backpack. And some stagger their classes so that one parent is always available for child care.

If your classes don't require you to be away from your baby for more than a few hours at a time, your breastfeeding schedule should not be interrupted. Or you may need to pump a few bottles a week or leave a few bottles of formula.

If you anticipate breastfeeding while in school, try to schedule your courses such that they are spread out over the day, allowing time between classes to go home or to the baby for feedings.

Bringing Baby to Work

Although some women do it—and do it well—having your baby with you at work all day is not as wonderful as it may sound. This arrangement puts a lot of demands on a mother, requiring her to have a sort of split personality: She must be "on call" to everyone, as she attempts to take care of her baby and get her work done, too.

Women who are able to manage this option successfully usually work out some arrangement to compensate their boss for "baby time" spent during the day. You can either deduct your "baby time" hours from your total work hours and charge only for the hours actually spent on the job, or you can go in early or stay later in the day to make up for your "baby time." Those mothers who are salaried employees or self-employed will be less likely to need such an arrangement, since their pay is not based specifically on hours worked; they work as long as it takes to get the job done, whether they spend a lot of "baby time" or not.

Have Pump, Will Travel

You certainly can travel and leave your baby at home if you need to, although it is not easy on mother, baby, or caregiver. And the longer you are away, the harder it will be. While you can be gone for a day, a few days, or even a week or more and still continue to breastfeed, long periods away from your baby have a negative impact on your milk supply and increase the difficulty of reinstating a good breastfeeding relationship upon your return. And the longer the separation, the greater the difficulty.

If you must travel, the ideal situation would be to take the baby with you. If you are traveling for work, this is rarely possible, and if it is possible, it will be more expensive, since you will have to bring along a caregiver. Even if you work all this out, the erratic trip schedule may complicate your life considerably, and you may end up pumping a lot anyway.

If you don't bring the baby along, you will need to pump almost around the clock in order to maintain your milk supply. Try to pump fairly close to the baby's regular nursing schedule. This will mean pumping in a lot of strange bathrooms. You will probably end up discarding this milk, heartbreaking as that may be. But it's just about impossible to store milk safely during a trip, and it would certainly be more work than it's worth. When you're on a trip, the purpose of pumping is to maintain your milk supply.

If you have been gone for two or more days, expect your milk supply to be low when you return. Nurse more for the first few days that you're home, and your supply will come back up again. The longer you have been away, the longer this readjustment will take. So if you are gone more than a couple of days, when you return, try to dedicate a few days to just nursing and resting.

Finding the Right Place

If you decide to nurse your baby during the day, while you're at work, your biggest task (other than securing permission from the management) will be to find an appropriate place to do so. If you can, arrange a quiet, private place that will always be available when you need it.

If you have to deal with less-than-perfect conditions, your plan to nurse during the workday may deteriorate quickly. For example, just consider yourself holding your crying baby in your arms, with people from the office all around, while you wait for the meeting in the conference room to break so that you can go in and nurse. You will feel helpless and frustrated on all levels: Being responsible for this disruption in the workplace will make you feel like a bad employee, and making your hungry baby to wait to nurse will make you feel like a bad mother.

Under good conditions, many mothers delight in this opportunity to spend some time with their babies during the day. Most women feel relaxed and refreshed after nursing and may even be more prepared to face the remaining day's work. Nursing provides a good break.

If you are unable to make arrangements to nurse at work, keep in mind that there are other possibilities. Work isn't the only place to nurse a baby! If your caregiver is close enough to your workplace, you may go to your baby over

You can nurse discreetly, without exposing your breast. Pull your blouse up from the bottom, instead of unbuttoning it from the top. With experience, you will gradually feel comfortable nursing in public.

your lunch break or during another time of day. Although there may be other disruptions at the caregiver's, in general, you will probably be more comfortable at the caregiver's than at work.

Some mothers love this midday time with their baby. And again, it's a good break from work. It's also a good chance to get to know the caregiver who plays such a big role in your baby's life. However, some mothers find that seeing the baby during the day only means that they'll have to be separated one more time. If this additional separation is too hard on either mother or baby, this nursing option is just not for you. You will do better to spend your break time from work pumping another bottle.

Pumping

The ideal place for a woman to pump while at work is a clean, comfortable women's lounge. It will have a good chair or sofa, a sink, and an electrical outlet. A luxurious lounge will even have a place to store a pump and other supplies, and the company refrigerator will be nearby.

Now let's come back to the real world. Actually, women have pumped in supply rooms, department store dressing rooms, closets, private offices, and many, many bathrooms, of all shapes and sizes. All you **really** need is some privacy.

The place in which you pump will affect your practical ability to pump enough milk, your attitude about pumping, and your colleagues' attitudes about it, as well. Most women simply use the restroom. If you do, see if you can put a comfortable chair in there. It will make pumping time much more relaxing.

Breastfeeding Etiquette

There is continual controversy over the issue of nursing in public. Many people are highly offended by a woman nursing her baby in a department store or restaurant. Still others are outraged by stories of women arrested for breastfeeding in public. There seems to be no middle ground in this controversy.

The basis of the debate, of course, is that some people think of breasts in a private or sexual way, while others think of them for feeding infants. Fortunately, little by little, our society is coming to accept breastfeeding as a normal, natural means of feeding a baby.

Every baby has the right to be fed when hungry, and feeding usually can't be put off until a more convenient time. What's more, you have the right to feed your baby when and where you choose. But consider that you also have an opportunity to promote positive attitudes toward breastfeeding.

If you choose to breastfeed in a place where other people may see you, do it discreetly. It is entirely possible—easy in fact—to nurse in such a way that the baby's mouth covers your nipple and your blouse drapes down to cover the rest of your breast. Passersby would find it difficult to tell if you were breast-feeding or simply cuddling your baby.

The value of discreet public nursing is twofold. First and most important, you will be able to meet your baby's needs by nursing whenever he's hungry. And second, you will help effect much needed social change toward acceptance of breastfeeding.

Your employment, however, is another matter. Don't assume that you can nurse at work **except** in complete privacy, with management approval. Even if you are the boss and have the authority, carefully consider your profes-sional image with clients and employees.

Most women who pump or nurse at work do their best to be as private as pos-sible. Professionally, women do not want to damage their image and thus jeopardize their careers; there is simply no need to risk making those around you uncomfortable. And personally, women feel that how they choose to feed their baby is a private matter. Whose business is it, anyway?

The Law and Breastfeeding

Consider the following cases:

A woman, herself highly allergic, felt very strongly that she must breastfeed her child to help prevent him from developing similar allergic reactions. The baby re-fused to drink from a bottle (which would've allowed her to pump milk to leave for him during the day), so she asked for an extended leave from her job in order to continue nursing at home. Leave was denied.

Another mother, a teacher, was denied permission to nurse her baby at school over her lunch break, based on a school board policy prohibiting teachers from bringing their children to school. When the baby subsequently developed a for-mula allergy, the mother requested permission to nurse in a trailer in the school parking lot. This, too, was denied, based on another policy prohibiting teachers from leaving the premises during the day.

Linda Eaton, a firefighter in Iowa, fought and finally won permission to have her baby brought to her during her work breaks in order to nurse in the women's locker room. However, Linda ended up resigning because of continued harass-ment over the issue. (For more on this case, see Chapter 8, p. 123.)

All of these are actual cases, ending with very mixed and, for the most part, inconclusive results.

Sadly, American society does not support the needs of families very well. Some countries have national daycare policies and even policies specifically designed to support breastfeeding, such as on-site daycare and scheduled nursing breaks. But the United States has no national daycare policy, paternity leaves are rare, and even maternity leaves are seldom adequate to support the needs of young families. Although we now have some rights and protection regarding pregnancy, birth, and maternity leave, there are still no specific legal provisions for breastfeeding women.

Because of this legal shortcoming, each case is decided by interpreting existing laws to include breastfeeding. And because the whole issue of breastfeeding and working is relatively new, very few cases have been tried, which means there is little legal precedence. Finally, because of the pressures that parents face in separating work and family, most employed mothers who experience breastfeeding difficulties simply give up nursing instead of challenging the system. For all of these reasons, it will most likely be some time before there is sufficient legal protection for breastfeeding women.

To date, there are three possible legal approaches, each of which has been interpreted to provide a general foundation for the right to breastfeed: (1) Title VII of the Civil Rights Act of 1964, (2) the Constitution, and (3) the Pregnancy Discrimination act of 1978. We will discuss each in turn.

Title VII of the Civil Rights Act of 1964. Most women presume that their right to breastfeed is protected by the laws regarding discrimination based on sex, but in reality, that may not be the case. Title VII is the federal law prohibiting discrimination in employment practices based on race, color, religion, sex, or national origin. Any employer, private or government, of 15 or more employees must comply with Title VII mandates.

Title VII makes it illegal to discriminate by sex in any of three ways:

1. through basic policies that treat men differently than women based on sex;

2. through disparate impact policies, which cause discrimination through such things as height and weight requirements that obviously single out one or the other sex; and

3. through disparate treatment practices, which include instances where women are treated differently than men in spite of policies that don't discriminate.

The purpose of Title VII is to provide equal treatment in the workplace for men and women. But the definition of "equal treatment" is open to interpretation. For instance, since only women can breastfeed, it is difficult to find discrimination, based on the policies outlined above. On the other hand, if employment policies prohibit breastfeeding, the employer may effectively exclude women from the workplace, which is discrimination through disparate treatment.

Keep in mind that these are only interpretations, not legal precedents. Thus, while most women presume that their right to breastfeed is protected by the laws regarding discrimination based on sex, in reality, this may not be the case. Simply put, it has not yet been established that an employer preventing a woman from breastfeeding constitutes sexual discrimination.

The Constitution. A second approach is based on the legal protection provided by the Ninth and Fourteenth Amendments to the Constitution.

The Ninth Amendment states:

The enumeration in the Constitution of certain rights shall not be construed to deny or disparage others retained by the people.

In plain English, this means that you can't use one part of the Constitution to deny anyone other rights listed in the Constitution.

Section 1 of the Fourteenth Amendment states:

All persons born or naturalized in the United States, and subject to the jurisdiction thereof, are citizens of the United States and of the state wherein they reside. No state shall make or enforce any law which shall abridge the privileges or immunities of citizens of the United States; nor shall any state deprive any person of life, liberty, or property, without due process of law; nor deny to any person within its jurisdiction the equal rights or equal protection of the law.

Simply put, states cannot deprive citizens of their equal rights.

There is some precedent to establish breastfeeding as a "fundamental right" that is protected by the Constitution. One case involving a government worker did find that the state, as the employer, could not deny the right to breastfeed, since it is a "fundamental right." So anyone employed by a state in any capacity whose fundamental right to breastfeed was being denied could allege that the state was denying her rights. Thus far, private-sector employees have not been granted this protection; government employees have a little more hope.

The Pregnancy Discrimination Act of 1978. The Pregnancy Discrimination Act (PDA) forbids discrimination due to "pregnancy, childbirth and related conditions" and is the legal basis requiring that maternity leaves be equal to other disability leaves. Had anyone anticipated the need, this is probably where the legalities of breastfeeding should have been covered.

While one might easily consider breastfeeding to be a "related condition" to childbirth, this has not been established legally. Should this happen, the protection afforded would be considerable. For the PDA mandates that employers treat an employee who is temporarily unable to perform her duties due to her pregnancy-related condition in the same manner that they treat other disabled employees. As we discussed in Chapter 3, the PDA does not require an employer to adopt specific policies, but it does require that their disability policy includes pregnancy-related conditions. Depending on existing company policies, this could mean provisions for leave, changes in hours or duties, or other individual accommodations to avoid discrimination.

On the Horizon

One bright spot on the horizon, for both families and children, is the Parental and Disability Leave Act of 1985 (H.R. 2020), which was introduced by Congresswoman Pat Schroeder (Colorado). Although not yet passed into law, this bill provides specific protection for both mothers and fathers, including longer leaves with guaranteed benefits for parents in cases of birth, adoption, or the serious illness of a child.

Although this legislation does not address the issue of breastfeeding and employment, it does begin to repair the split in the lives of employed parents by acknowledging that the workplace can indeed support family life.

Practically Speaking

So, we've established that there is no specific legal protection for the employed, breastfeeding mother. In the meantime, what can you do if you find yourself in a discriminatory situation?

Step 1. Begin to keep a daily journal of events and conversations that seem relevant to the discrimination. Don't depend on your memory. Write everything down, in your own handwriting.

Step 2. Consult your company's management or personnel department to get clear and accurate information about policies, precedents, and other creative solutions. Be sure you have all the facts.

If your company has a policy or procedure for filing a grievance, try following the system. You will probably be required to have exhausted all available remedies before initiating legal action.

Step 3A. Some would recommend that you proceed immediately to Step 3B (below), which is filing your complaint with the Equal Employment Opportunity Commission (EEOC). But we feel that, if you have gone this far and not resolved the problem, you should consult an attorney.

Granted, attorneys are expensive, and you can file an EEOC complaint without legal counsel. However, there are advantages to seeking legal counsel early in the process:

• A letter from your attorney to your employer will demonstrate that you are serious about the matter and may even magically bring about a prompt decision in your favor.

• A good attorney who is versed in discrimination law in your area can help you decide if you should really file a complaint against your employer. Should you decide to file, an attorney can also recommend whether to file with the EEOC or your state agency.

- Finally, an attorney will be aware of the time restrictions for filing a complaint, which vary from 180 days to 300 days from the alleged discrimination, depending on your state's laws and the agency handling the charge. These time restrictions are very important.

It is not always easy to find a good attorney. Recommendations from friends are only valuable if they refer you to an attorney who specializes in civil rights law. Thus, your neighbor's divorce lawyer will probably not be suitable for your discrimination case. Referrals from your regular attorney (if you have one) to someone experienced in civil rights are worth considering. Your local Women's Bar Association may also prove helpful, particularly since yours will be a women's rights case. And the EEOC or comparable state agency may make referrals, as well.

If you are willing to do a little research, you may be able to find out which attorneys in your area have handled recent civil rights cases (hopefully, with some success). News clippings at the library or the clerk at the courthouse may help you track down some names.

Anyone who has been involved in the legal process will tell you that having the right attorney can be as or more important to the outcome of your case than the issues themselves. So before you hire anyone, be direct and ask how much civil rights experience he or she has had. Finding the right attorney can affect not only the outcome but the price tag, as well. Someone inexperienced at civil rights law may spend far more research hours on your case than an experienced attorney would.

If your case is very strong, you may find an attorney who will work on a contingency basis. But most likely, you will have to pay a retainer up front and make additional payments as the case proceeds. On the bright side, if you win your case, the party you sue (or the party charged in your complaint) can be required to pay your legal fees.

Step 3B. Whether you hire an attorney or not, your next step will be to file a complaint against your employer. Again, you do not have to be represented by an attorney to file a complaint. But an attorney's assistance will be valuable in deciding where to file.

The Equal Employment Opportunity Commission (EEOC), which was created by Congress to enforce Title VII, has the authority to file suit on your behalf in Federal District Court. Your state may also have a Fair Employment Practices Agency or a Civil Rights Commission that handles discrimination cases on the state level. Your state agency may work closely with the local EEOC office, automatically filing every case with both agencies to avoid redundancy. So choose the right agency, the EEOC or your state equivalent, and file a formal complaint.

Locate your local EEOC office in the telephone directory under "U.S. Government Offices." You can call initially to ask questions and provide basic intake information, but, at some point, you will be required to go in and sign the charges. The EEOC can offer advice about the strength of your case, but they cannot refuse to file your complaint, even if they think your case is weak. (The complaint process is different for federal employees; your EEOC office can advise you.)

The EEOC will notify your employer that you have made a complaint. You should know that you have certain protections from being fired, reassigned, demoted, or otherwise harassed. The EEOC will then act as mediator, holding a fact-finding conference and possibly investigating further.

Your employer can offer to settle at any point in the process; the settlement between you and your employer would be negotiated by the EEOC (and possibly your attorney, if you have hired one). If, after the entire EEOC process, you and your employer have not come to agreement, you will be issued a right-to-sue notice, which means that you can take your case to court—and start all over again!

The Settlement. Whether you settle through the EEOC or in court, by the end of this process, you will most likely feel that you deserve the moon and the stars when it comes time to settle. Restrain yourself!

Title VII spells out the variety of settlements possible, including the following:

• that your employer end the discriminatory practices;

• that you be reinstated, promoted, or transferred, as deemed appropriate for the situation;

• that you receive back pay and benefits, including such things as leave, overtime, and vacation pay;

• that your seniority be restored; and

• that new affirmative action policies be established to end discrimination against women in the workplace.

A Final Word of Advice

Perhaps the best strategy to follow, should you need to take any legal action, is to stall for time. This was the approach used by the attorney for Linda Eaton, the firefighter we mentioned earlier. Linda and her attorney filed for an injunction to stop the city from punishing Linda, and a restraining order was issued so Linda could continue to work and breastfeed, as she had planned to, until a trial could be held.

Litigation can take years, while breastfeeding lasts only a short time and can't be put off. Working and breastfeeding is difficult enough, without adding the stress of a legal action, too. If possible, take care of the breastfeeding now and the legal debate later. Time is on your side.

Summary

While it may seem very taxing to pump and/or nurse at work, remember that it is very temporary. Depending on how old your baby is when you go back to work, you will probably only need to pump at work for a few months. By the time your baby is six months old, he will begin to take solids and juice at the caregiver's, so you won't need to supply as much milk. And sometime during the second six months of your baby's life, you will be able to stop pumping altogether. He will be receiving even more solid foods and juice at the caregiver's, and you will continue to nurse when you are with him.

Don't let all of the many considerations overwhelm you. Remember that every situation is different, and only you can decide on the best arrangement for you. While making this decision, keep the following guidelines in mind:

• Take as long a maternity leave as possible. It is better to be ready to go back early and be pleasantly surprised than to feel rushed and return to work frustrated and tired.

• When you do return to work, ease back into your schedule, if you can. Try to avoid taking on any extra duties and travelling for awhile.

• If your schedule is flexible, take your pumping or nursing breaks as you need them. If your schedule is not flexible, use your breaks and lunch hour to pump or nurse, or consider giving the baby formula while you are at work and continue to breastfeed only when you're home.

• Although some situations may seem ideal—including bringing your baby to work, working at home, and going to the baby to nurse—they all include psychological and emotional pressures.

A final word on the legal front: Although there is presently no specific legal protection for employed, breastfeeding women, it seems likely that positive legal decisions will be forthcoming and thus set precedence for breastfeeding issues. Such decisions will not only benefit breastfeeding women but parents and families in general.

Chapter 8

Choices, Choices, Choices

Not all employed mothers work from nine to five, Monday through Friday. Some work around schedules that are nearly incompatible with breastfeeding and require a lot of careful planning. Others purposefully choose an alternative work schedule that makes their breastfeeding a lot easier.

If you need to find an alternative, explore the possibilities. In this chapter, we will look at the following work arrangements and their implications for breastfeeding:

- rotating shift work;
- nursing at lunch;
- part-time work (long-shift, short-shift);
- job sharing;
- working freelance;
- working at home; and
- bringing your baby to work.

Around the World

A great way to review your work alternatives is to look at how other cultures view the issue of employed, nursing mothers.

In Israel, almost every mother is an employed mother. Although breastfeeding is not as popular in Israel as it is in the United States, there is official encouragement for Israelis to nurse. An Israeli La Leche League leader, Toby Gish, shared the following information about employed, nursing mothers in Israel:

Israeli women have a three-month paid maternity leave, and when they return to work, they can work an hour less each day for the same pay if they are breastfeeding.

More and more Israeli women are electing to continue to breastfeed when they return to work for several reasons. First is their reluctance to leave the nursing experience. Second, it's some emotional compensation for leaving the baby. Third, there is increased public awareness of the importance of breastfeeding due to La Leche League, newspaper articles, etc. Fourth is the availability and popularity of the Kaneson Expressing and Feeding Bottle for a reasonable price. [The Kaneson system was the only pump available in Israel at that time.]

Most Israeli mothers are absent for only one or two feedings. There are those who elect to pump and leave a bottle of mother's milk for the metapelet [babysitter] to give the baby. Some choose to replace one meal for older babies with a fruit meal and others leave a bottle of formula.

Some women are finding other solutions. Lisa has received permission from the manager of the bank where she works to have her daughter brought to her for a nursing break instead of a coffee break. Her manager even offered her the use of his office. Ruthi took Elisheva back to the university with her. Donna Ron, [a] Kibbutznick La Leche League leader, kept the Kibbutz switchboard running for seven months with her son happily stretched out on a blanket next to her. The best endorsement for the magic of a happy breastfeeding experience here are these mothers who are finding ingenious ways to stretch their maternity leaves.

Looking at the Alternatives

When women are faced with a conflict between what they need—a job and income—and what they want badly—the opportunity to continue to nurse their babies—they can be most creative in making compromises and reaching solutions. In the following sections, we will share some of the alternatives that other women have found. Each arrangement involves its own set of breastfeeding issues, including basic pros and cons and management techniques.

Perhaps one of these alternatives may fit your situation and will appeal to you. Or perhaps hearing other people's ideas and flexible solutions will encourage you to develop your own solution, the one that is best-suited to your life.

Rotating Shift Work

Rotating shift work will affect your milk supply very differently depending on whether your shift rotates every few days or less often (weekly, montly, etc.).

Due to the supply and demand nature of milk supply, employed mothers with regular hours get less full at work, unless they pump often and effectively. The woman who rotates shifts frequently will probably not experience this less-full/more-full cycle, since there is no **regular** period when her breasts receive more or less stimulation.

A more-full period becomes established when the breast is stimulated (through nursing or pumping) repeatedly at a regular time; a less-full period is established at a time when the breast receives little or no regular stimulation. For most employed, nursing women, these periods occur at consistent times: less stimulation during the work day and more on off-work hours. But for a woman working rotating shifts, these times aren't consistent.

For that reason—**no consistent conditioning**—the shift worker probably won't be more full at one time of day and less full at another. If, however, she works the same shift for a whole week, she'll probably find the full- and less-full times beginning to emerge—just as she changes shifts. Now the time the baby used to nurse is the time she's at work, away from her baby. Her body will still fill with milk, so she'll need to express her breasts to relieve the fullness, whether or not she's providing pumped breast milk for her baby. Pumping at work will also help keep her supply up.

Another concern for the mother who works rotating shifts is the fact that she may have different supervisors for the different shifts she works. Some supervisors may be more or less supportive than others of pumping and any other arrangements that are made, like having the baby brought in to nurse on break. The mother who works various shifts should discuss any special needs with the supervisor of each shift she works.

Lee works rotating shifts at a local factory. The first difficulty she encountered was that, as a single mother, she needed child care for all the shifts she worked. Lee ended up with three separate child care arrangements, one for each shift. When she works days, her babysitter and supervisor both agreed to having her baby brought to work and nursed at lunch. When she works evenings and nights, she pumps (which she did not feel required any supervisor notification or approval) and stores her milk in the refrigerator in the employees' lounge. Lee doesn't feel that her rotating shift work is unusually difficult. She likes the fact that she is sometimes able to work during her baby's sleeping hours.

Nursing at Lunch

Some women do not want to be separated from their newborn babies for eight or nine hours at a time and do not want to pump at work, either. These women have come up with ways to nurse their babies during the work day. In order to do so, both their work time and workplace have had to be flexible.

Laurel, who works in a bank, told us:

I made an arrangement with my supervisor that allowed me to combine my two 15-minute breaks with my half-hour lunch break, so I could take an hour at lunch time. This gave me time to drive to my babysitter's house. Fortunately, I was able to find a sitter who lived close to work and who didn't mind my daily visit. I nursed Jeremy from about 8:30 until 8:45 at the babysitter's before I left; then I nursed him again at about 12:15 and spent the rest of our time together holding, cuddling, rocking, playing with him, or whatever he seemed to want.

This was necessary for me. I simply could not bear that much time away from my baby. I have heard other women say that two separations in one day makes it harder for them or for the baby, but it didn't work that way for us. My baby greatly enjoyed our time together, and it relieved my guilt feelings somewhat. Jeremy usually took a nap after I left and then took a bottle about 3:00 or 4:00 and nursed again eagerly shortly after 6:00 when I returned. If it hadn't been for this arrangement with my understanding and cooperative babysitter, I don't know what I would have done!

Jeanne, a psychiatric resident, lives very close to the hospital at which she works. Because of this proximity, she hired a babysitter to come into her home. She then manages to go home often enough to nurse her baby exclusively and never has to leave any bottles.

Mary, an executive producer at a local TV station, has been successful in combining two arrangements: going home to nurse the baby during lunch and having the baby brought to her. Mary hired a nanny so her two daughters can stay home. She nurses her infant at about 7:00 a.m. each morning, before she goes to work. On most days, she leaves work at 11:30 and comes home to nurse her baby again. On those days that Mary cannot leave the station, the nanny brings the baby to her, and she nurses at work. Mary nurses for 40 minutes each time, and the baby seems quite full afterward. Sometimes the nanny feeds the baby a bottle of expressed breast milk between nursings; other times, the baby does not seem hungry until her mother appears.

Mary says that 99 percent of her co-workers are supportive of her nursing, but she has received occasional criticism. Her supervisor is completely supportive, however, and that has certainly been an element in her success.

Many celebrities follow a variation of Mary's arrangement: They hire a nanny to come to work with the baby. This allows them great flexibility for breastfeeding, as well as play and other care. Many well-known personalities—including Lynn Redgrave, Marriette Hartley, Joan Lunden, and Goldie Hawn—have made extra efforts in order to breastfeed their babies. So has actress Jaclyn Smith, as reported in a *Time* magazine article:

Although she [Smith] has not yet chosen a project, she is adamant about breast-feeding on the set. "I'll convert my trailer into a nursery," she says. It may complicate her life, but Smith believes the enrichment outweighs the disadvantages. (Time, February 22, 1982)

You may have heard or read about Linda Eaton, the firefighter from Iowa, who received enormous publicity in early 1979 because she arranged to have her son, Ian (then three months old), brought to her at work for breastfeeding. Linda only nursed on her personal time, a period during which other co-workers also received visits from their families. Yet she was fired over this issue.

Linda took her case before the Civil Rights Commission, who concluded that the city's action was based upon "opposition to the physical act of breastfeeding." The Commission ruled that "singling out an employee for different treatment because of the employee's breastfeeding is discriminating on the basis of sex." Linda was awarded $2,000 for emotional stress, $145 for back wages, and $26,442 in attorney's fees. Although Linda did go back to work, she resigned two weeks after the Commission's ruling because of harassment and pranks from her fellow firefighters. (See the September 1980 issue of *MS* for more on this case.)

Although most of us will not meet the extreme opposition that Linda Eaton faced, we will probably not be able to afford hiring a nanny to accompany us to work, either. Unfortunately, even the practical application of going to your baby during lunch has both drawbacks and benefits.

The biggest drawback is inconvenience, since you must make special arrangements in your schedule and travel to and from the baby. You may actually end up working a longer day in order to have enough break and lunch time to travel and nurse.

The most obvious benefit of arranging to nurse during your workday is that you can probably avoid the nuisance of pumping at work. Nursing at work is also a real plus for the baby, since she receives the extra physical and emotional contact with her mother. And the fact that you are nursing instead of pumping will definitely help you maintain your milk supply more easily. Although pumping can be effective, there is really no substitute for having your baby at your breast.

Evaluate this alternative according to your own preferences and priorities, as well as the needs and personality of your baby. We recommend nursing at work to the woman who is highly opposed to pumping at work, who wishes to give her baby nothing but breast milk, and whose caregiver is conveniently located. This may also be a solution for the woman whose baby refuses a bottle. However, nursing at work is not a good choice for a woman whose schedule includes sporadic lunch times and breaks or when making the arrangements with work and a babysitter cause too much tension.

Part-time Work

Part-time work can be a temporary or a permanent compromise with motherhood. If you do decide to go part-time, you will undoubtedly have an easier time breastfeeding than if you work full-time. You can take the advice and information we give about nursing while working full-time and cut it back to fit your own needs. Depending on how many hours you work each day, you might not have to pump at all.

Dottie Lamm, a popular columnist in the *Denver Post* and former First Lady of the state of Colorado, told us of her part-time work arrangement when she was breastfeeding her son, Scott:

I had a part-time job which was generally 13½ hours a week, but sometimes it was extended to 20. Either way, I was able to miss only one feeding each day I worked, and I only worked three days a week. At the age of six weeks, I began to get Scott used to a substitute formula feeding for the times I would be gone. He didn't like it the first time, but the second time he gobbled it up eagerly. So I felt very relieved and free to go back to work at seven weeks, as I had planned. I never used a breast pump because I only missed one feeding and didn't find it necessary. Also, I felt it was very good for him to have adapted to both breast and bottle milk, so occasionally on non-workdays my husband and I could go out in the evening and have another babysitter give him a substitute bottle. However, during the time I was breastfeeding and working, we did not go out very much, because I felt very strongly that the breastfeeding should predominate.

Another successful example of a mother who managed to work part-time while breastfeeding is Sharmon. She continued to teach religious school three afternoons a week for three hours each day after her baby was born. She nursed Emily when she dropped her off at her mother-in-law's house and then again as soon as she returned from work. With this arrangement, Sharmon never had to pump a single bottle.

Some women have the option of simply cutting back the number of hours they work. For instance, if you are in a private, professional practice, you may be able to adjust your schedule to meet your new priorities by taking fewer clients.

If you don't have this choice, talk to your employer about working fewer hours. Patty, a social worker, explains how she made such an arrangement:

After Ricky was born, I took a couple of months off work. Instead of going back to 40 hours a week, I asked for only 20 hours a week. As Ricky got a little older and started taking more solids, by about nine months, I didn't need to leave as much breast milk for him. At that point, I went up to 30 hours a week.

Working part-time and combining some of the other alternatives presented in this chapter might work well for you, too. For example, Sally, a nurse-practitioner at a birthing center, took on fewer clients after the birth of her own child. And when she worked, she took the baby with her to see patients until she felt the baby was old enough for more structured daycare.

If your part-time work involves just a few hours each day, you may not need to pump milk or leave formula at all. You may be able to nurse your baby before and after work and eventually add juice and solids.

If your part-time job involves a full day, several days a week, you will be able to keep up your milk supply by nursing full-time on your days off and pumping when you are at work. If you want to leave formula, you may find that you need to pump a little at work to relieve the fullness, since your breasts will be used to filling with milk during those hours.

Like any alternative, part-time work has its pros and cons. The main disadvantage is that you will earn less money than if you work full-time. However, you will also be spending less on daycare. In addition, reducing your job to part-time may mean passing up promotions and raises. And depending on your particular job, reducing your hours may or may not be practical.

The advantages of having extra time off will be very special for both you and your baby, which may help alleviate your feelings of guilt and anxiety over working less. Naturally, you will need to do less pumping or perhaps none at all. Since you will be nursing more, your milk supply will be more easily maintained. But the most important advantage of all is, of course, the extra time for contact with your baby.

Job Sharing

Another possibility for part-time work is job sharing. Under this arrangement, two individuals split the hours and work usually done by a single person, creating two jobs where there was originally just one. For instance, the job could be split by having each individual work a half-day or even a half-week. Two teachers in Denver split a teaching job by taking six-week turns.

In addition to the practical convenience it offers, job sharing also solves an economic problem associated with part-time work. It seems to be an economic fact that part-time work pays less per hour than full-time work, regardless of the training or position. But when one full-time job is split into two part-time jobs, the full-time wage is normally split in two, as well. The result is that working part-time through job sharing pays better than regular part-time work.

Job sharing is a fairly new idea and has not been used extensively. Although it may be unfeasible for some jobs, it works well in many trades and most clerical positions, as well as some professional practices. Even though job sharing may not have been tried at your workplace before, it doesn't mean that it's out of the question. Approach the management and discuss a job-sharing arrangement, especially if you know someone who would be interested in splitting a job with you.

Working Freelance

Another variation of part-time employment is working freelance. If you want to work less than regular, full-time hours yet keep one foot in the work world, examine your skills and see if they can be restructured to create a freelance job. For example, can you take what you've been doing at work for your employer and do it at home for yourself?

We know of a landscape architect and a women who does public relations and editing who have both done this very successfully. Some nurses now work freelance by doing physicals for insurance companies at their own convenience, rather than work in more traditional nursing jobs. And Anne Price, coauthor of this book, used her prior experience as a secondary school teacher to develop part-time teaching work after her children were born. Anne has taught speed reading, the Red Cross Babysitting course, various other courses, and substituted in the public schools. Clearly, many other professions also lend themselves to freelance work. The possibilities are really endless.

Right after your baby's birth, you may be able to keep her with you at work, since newborns usually sleep a lot and require little entertainment. Later, as your baby becomes more demanding (and depending on your type of work), you may need to use a babysitter. However, you will be the one deciding on the time and amount of daycare.

Even if you can't go completely freelance, try bringing some of your work home with you to cut down on out-of-home hours. For instance, work that involves typing, working on a computer, writing, or reading could just as well be done at home, rather than at the office.

Working at Home

Working at home certainly offers more flexibility than most office-centered jobs. But, as we discussed in the last chapter, as perfect as this situation sounds for those lucky women who can arrange it, some difficulties must still be addressed.

If you work at home, you will probably have to meet with clients there. Thus, you may need some child care, at least a "mother's helper," to cover these meeting times, as well as any intense work periods. This will probably mean preparing some bottles of either breast milk or formula.

Another potential problem is a psychological one: It is often difficult to draw a clear line between "work time" and "mother time." You may end up frustrated, feeling that you can't devote enough time to either your work or your child. You may also get a case of "cabin fever," which afflicts many people who work in their homes; it's very easy to feel confined and even reclusive.

And once you have a baby, it will be even harder to leave the house. You might wish you could go to an office for a few hours a day.

Rather than let yourself be overcome by these difficulties, keep in mind the advantages that working at home provides. It enables you to keep working while also caring for your child in your own home. This arrangement gives you flexibility and control that other work situations can't offer.

You may choose to work at home on a permanent basis, or you may choose to do it temporarily as a way of easing back into working at the office. Mary, a TV producer, worked at home for the first six months after her baby was born. For her, this arrangement provided a transitional phase between the birth and going back to work "at work."

Bringing the Baby to Work

Another alternative is to bring your baby with you to work. Although this option is not feasible for many women, those who have a sufficiently flexible work situation find it very worthwhile.

This arrangement works best with a newborn baby, who pretty much sleeps and eats. And since leaving the baby during these first few months causes the mother the most anxiety, this is a good time to bring the baby along to work. Depending on where you work and what you do, you may be able to keep bringing your baby indefinitely. Just consider that, as your baby grows, she will sleep less and become more active, which may require you to adapt your plans somewhat.

We have spoken to many women who have taken their babies to work— some, successfully, others, not so successfully. Our discussion with these mothers brought out some experiences worth sharing.

Usually, the first thing that comes to the employer's mind is the possibility that your bringing your baby to work will cost him or her money. One an- swer to this objection is suggested by Diana Korte in her article "Baby on the Job," in *Colorado Woman* magazine. Diana refers to a Boulder mother of four, Pat, who works in a bakery. Pat simply charges her employer a flat fee for her work, rather than an hourly wage or a salary. This way, Pat's nursing her baby on the job is not a disadvantage to her employer. She just stays at work until she is finished with everything. Korte also reports that other women keep track of their "baby time" and either work extra hours to make it up or subtract the "baby hours" from their total hours on the job.

Nancy Dana, coauthor of this book, tried taking her two boys (then ages nine months and two years) with her to her part-time bookkeeping job. Although Nancy had her employer's blessing, she found it difficult to accomplish her work with the boys there. The boys' ages and the fact that there were two children involved certainly contributed to the difficulty of the situation. Nancy comments:

It was too hard for me emotionally. I was paid by the hour for working hours, and could really feel free to take as many baby hours as I cared to spend. But I always ended up feeling like I was cheating my boss by playing with the boys or that I was cheating the children by doing my job. Although the situation was ideal, the arrangement, for me, was mentally unfeasible. [P.S. The employer's wife now takes their baby with her and does the bookkeeping.]

Rhoda, who held a high-ranking position in a community center, found that she had no trouble bringing her infant daughter to work. She kept a travel bed in her office and was easily able to nurse without interruption, thanks to the privacy of her office.

Joan Lunden, cohost of "Good Morning, America," has managed to combine motherhood with a very demanding career. In her forward to the book *Of Cradles and Careers*, she writes of her experiences:

I had not planned to take Jamie to work with me, but as time drew near, it seemed to be the only answer.

I can't honestly tell you that it was easy. Bundling a baby at 4 a.m. to take her out into the cold morning air, feedings between tapings, and trying to maintain some decorum in my office—which now included baby swings, cribs, and changing tables. It was a difficult juggling act. But boy, was it worth it!

I can't possibly imagine not having had that unbelievable bond that breastfeeding developed. In those early months there was that first communication with my baby, her gorgeous, dark eyes looking up into mine silently saying, "I need you!" Those eyes were my constant reminders that what I was doing was the right thing.

The September 1980 issue of *MS* reports the case of Barbara Koser, of Eugene, Oregon, who was an administrative clerk for the Census Bureau. Barbara began bringing her son, Jefferson, to work with her when he was one week old. She had no difficulty caring for Jefferson at work or managing her duties on the job. But shortly after she began this practice, the acting manager sent a memo saying that she could no longer bring her baby to work. The reason cited was that the baby was not covered by worker's compensation and the Bureau didn't want to be open to a possible lawsuit.

Barbara took a very creative approach to this problem. She took her case to Northwest Legal Advocates, a nonprofit, public interest law firm in Eugene. They helped her draft a document that exempted the Census Bureau from liability should Jefferson be injured while with his mother at work. The Bureau accepted this document, and Jefferson was "back at work" in just a little over two weeks.

Of course, working in a profession that offers the possibilities of self-determined hours and a private office is ideal if you want to bring your baby to work. Similarly, being self-employed or high up in management also eliminates some ticklish problems with securing your employer's permission.

Georgann, a chiropractor, has her own practice and brings her infant son, Russell, to work with her. Obviously, Georgann does not have to worry about her supervisor's reaction to this arrangement; instead, she must be concerned with her receptionist's reaction. Georgann must rely on her receptionist to care for the baby when she is with a patient, but she doesn't feel it is fair to expect this "extra duty" from her employee. In order to compensate the receptionist fairly, Georgann pays her her regular salary, plus a child care fee based on the number of hours the receptionist spends taking care of the baby.

Another mother, Pat, was pleasantly surprised when her employer, Planned Parenthood, suggested that she bring her baby to work, remarking that "if Planned Parenthood can't handle it, who can?" Although this arrangement was not without difficulty, Pat reports in *Working Woman* that the experience was a positive one for all concerned—even her co-workers. She writes:

When my door was closed, the staff gave me complete privacy. An open door was an invitation for them to take the baby, which gave me a break and them a breather from their jobs. There was never any shortage of takers. "He's a great stress reliever," a financial assistant remarked.

While many women are successful in taking their babies to work, it is undoubtedly difficult to satisfy both the baby's needs and the demands of the job in one time slot. For many mothers, it is comparable to working two full-time jobs at once.

Still, this arrangement remains attractive to those women who feel strongly about being separated from their babies. One of these mothers summed it up this way: "I don't want to miss a moment of my baby's life. If I'm going to have babies, I don't have to leave them just because I have to work."

Another advantage of bringing your baby to work is the elimination of costly child care fees, which means you will be able to take home more of your earnings. And needless to say, a mother who takes her baby along has also eliminated worries over pumping, storing, and milk supply.

A creative compromise was developed by mother/attorney, Karen. Karen and her husband, a physician, purchased an office building and remodeled it, adding a daycare center for the tenants. Professionals—both mothers and fathers—who want to combine bringing their babies to work with a structured daycare situation are renting offices in this building. This is an ideal situation for a breastfeeding woman.

Summary

The variety of work situations that are possible for a breastfeeding mother are almost endless. Certainly, each situation has its own nursing issues, as well as advantages and disadvantages.

• Rotating shift work will probably make your milk supply ups and downs harder to predict, and you may have to make various daycare arrangements to meet your changing schedule.

• Nursing at lunch requires a good deal of flexibility and cooperation, but for those women who cannot bear to be separated from their babies, it's a good option.

• Part-time work will undoubtedly make breastfeeding easier, even if you do have to pump or use formula on occasion; consider making arrangements to work part-time even temporarily.

• Job sharing is a new option that combines the stability and economic advantages of full-time employment with the schedule advantages of part-time employment.

• Working freelance allows a mother to work less than full-time and at her own convenience; disadvantages include psychological pressures.

• Working at home, like working freelance, allows a mother to control when and how much she works; again, there may be psychological and logistic conflicts.

• Bringing the baby to work is a good option for those mothers who don't want to be separated from their children; the success of this option depends on your employer's attitude, the number and ages of your children, the type of work you do.

We hope that the examination of these working/mothering options will help you think creatively in making your own decision. Remember, there is no one right solution. And only you can decide what's right for you and your child.

Index

ORDER FORM

Qty.	Order #	Book Title	Author	Price
_____	1159	**Baby and Child Medical Care**	Hart, T..............	$ 5.95
_____	1039	**Baby Talk**	Lansky, B.	$ 4.95
_____	1239	**Best Baby Shower Book, The**..................	Cooke, C.	$ 4.95
_____	1029	**Best Baby Name Book, The**	Lansky, B.	$ 3.95
_____	1049	**David, We're Pregnant!**	Johnston, L.	$ 3.95
_____	1059	**Dear Babysitter**	Lansky, V.	$ 8.95
_____	1069	**Dear Babysitter Refill Pad**	Lansky, V.	$ 2.95
_____	1079	**Discipline Without Shouting or Spanking**	Wyckoff/Unell	$ 4.95
_____	1089	**Do They Ever Grow Up?**	Johnston, L.	$ 3.95
_____	1099	**Exercises for Baby & Me**	Regnier, S.	$ 9.95
_____	1109	**Feed Me! I'm Yours**	Lansky, V.	$ 6.95
_____	1119	**First-Year Baby Care**	Kelly, P.	$ 5.95
_____	1229	**Getting Organized For Your New Baby**.........	Bard, M.............	$ 4.95
_____	4009	**Grandma Knows Best**	McBride, M.	$ 4.95
_____	3109	**Grandma's Favorites Photo Album**	Meadowbrook	$ 6.50
_____	1139	**Hi Mom! Hi Dad!**	Johnston, L.	$ 3.95
_____	1149	**Mother Murphy's Law**	Lansky, B.	$ 2.95
_____	3129	**My First Five Years Record Book**	Meadowbrook	$11.95
_____	3119	**My First Year Calendar**	Meadowbrook	$ 7.95
_____	3139	**My First Year Photo Album**	Meadowbrook	$14.95
_____	3179	**Our Baby's First Year Calendar**	Meadowbrook	$ 7.95
_____	1179	**Practical Parenting Tips**	Lansky, V.	$ 6.95
_____	1169	**Pregnancy, Childbirth and the Newborn**	Simkin/Whalley	$ 9.95
_____	1199	**Successful Breastfeeding**	Dana/Price	$ 8.95
_____	1210	**10,000 Baby Names**..........................	Lansky, B.	$ 2.95
_____	1259	**Working Woman's Guide to Breastfeeding, The** .	Dana/Price	$ 6.95

Please send me copies of the books checked above. I am enclosing $ _____
which covers the full amount per book shown above plus $1.00 for postage and handling for
the first book and $.50 for each additional book. (Add $2.00 to total for postage and handling
for books shipped to Canada. Overseas postage and handling will be billed. MN residents
add 6% sales tax.) Allow up to four weeks for delivery. Quantity discounts available upon
request.

Send check or money order to Meadowbrook, Inc. No cash or C.O.D.s, please.

**For purchases over $10.00, you may use VISA or MasterCard (order by mail or phone). For
these orders we need information below.**

Charge to: ☐ **VISA**   ☐ **MasterCard**   Account # _____

Expiration Date _____

Card Signature _____

Send Book(s) to:

Name _____

Address _____

City _____ State _____ Zip _____

**Mail order to: Book Orders, Meadowbrook, Inc., 18318 Minnetonka Blvd., Deephaven, MN 55391,
Phone orders: (612) 473-5400, or Toll Free (800) 338-2232.**